Hunting—What Else

by

Dipl. Ing. FH Michael A. Engster

The contents of this work, including, but not limited to, the accuracy of events, people, and places depicted; opinions expressed; permission to use previously published materials included; and any advice given or actions advocated are solely the responsibility of the author, who assumes all liability for said work and indemnifies the publisher against any claims stemming from publication of the work.

All Rights Reserved
Copyright © 2019 by Michael Engster

No part of this book may be reproduced or transmitted, downloaded, distributed, reverse engineered, or stored in or introduced into any information storage and retrieval system, in any form or by any means, including photocopying and recording, whether electronic or mechanical, now known or hereinafter invented without permission in writing from the publisher.

Dorrance Publishing Co
585 Alpha Drive
Suite 103
Pittsburgh, PA 15238
Visit our website at *www.dorrancebookstore.com*

ISBN: 978-1-4809-8275-8
eISBN: 978-1-4809-8250-5

Introduction

I wrote this book because I love hunting. I also love telling stories at a campfire, and interacting with people of different countries, different religions, different colors, different education, different political views, etc.

At a campfire we are all the same. The paint comes off and we are just people who escaped our all too political world for a brief moment. Campfire talk includes a little bit of bragging about our hunting experiences, trophies are getting bigger, shots get longer but other than that it is honest.

Hunting creates a bond between us, it creates understanding, tolerance and friendship.

In a time where a non functioning cell phone is a disaster, kids interact by texting only, games are played inside the houses and heroes are science fiction figures, the contact to nature and the understanding of the outdoor world seems to fade away. In my mind, this is an utterly sad as well as dangerous development, and I hope that some of my stories might trigger a touch of interest in outdoor life.

Adventure is still out there but it is not found spending hours on the internet pushing buttons on a key board.

I also wrote this book for my children, grandkids ad for all those who do not have the opportunity, the physical ability, or just the drive to get out of the recliner and do what I did and still do. My hope is that they will get an inside look at a world that will eventually get smaller and smaller unless understanding of nature is rekindled.

And, like I said before: Adventure is still out there for those who dare!

Happy Trails,
Mike Engster

The horn of the hunter sounded early for me when my grandfather, Friedrich Wilhelm Seeburger, introduced me to hunting in post-World War II Germany. Food was scarce, and hunting was essential, as was poaching.

With the death of my grandfather came the death of hunting—at least for many years.

I heard the horn of the hunter again during my time in the Federal German Navy, but the sound was faint and did not really touch my heart until 1973, when I got my first legal German hunting license.

Ever since that moment, countless hours of intense pleasure, different places all over the world, and big and small adventures have made my life richer.

I hope that I will be able to pass some of our family's hunting heritage over to my sons.

Michael Engster
Dec. 2009
Osage County, Oklahoma

Date   : September 8, 1983
Location : Norway, Hardanger Joekulen Glacier Area
Hunters : Karl Gayer
             Stephan Engster
             Mike Engster

It is raining again, with a cold wind pushing dark clouds southeast. We are wet and hungry, and as the guide, I feel obligated to do something about it. And while I cannot change the Norwegian weather, I look for a spot out of the wind and get the small Coleman stove going.

Chicken noodle soup is on the menu, but when I serve it, the noodles still need some serious chewing. However, the "meal" is at least semi-warm. Nobody complains.

The weather turns from bad to worse and forces us back to the road where our car is parked. We drive to a place called Skulevikstoelen with the heater going full blast and wait for the weather to break. I turn the engine off and fall asleep.

It is about 3:00 p.m. when my son, Stephan, wakes me. The sun is shining, and we decide on a march to the Bjoreio River where Norwegian hunters did some serious shooting the day before. Reindeer like to walk into the wind, and we figure there is a chance of these animals coming back.

Further east, a big herd tried to cross the only street close to Halne Fjord. They were beat back by Norwegian road hunters.

It looks as though we might have a chance after all, and by the way, this is our last hunting day.

I follow Karl and Stephan, take some pictures, and start falling back a little. Suddenly, Stephan, who is the point-man, stops, gets on his knees, and motions us to be quiet.

On the other side of the little hill that we are about to cross is a whole heard of caribou/reindeer.

We do some belly crawling through wet grass and brush, and then I see them.

The picture is absolutely breathtaking. More than 200 reindeer are bunched up at a small pond right in front of us. I swear silently. A few hours ago, I shot a calf because of the meat, and now I have no license left.

But then again it is Karl's turn, anyway, so I put my gun aside and take pictures. Karl tries to sneak up on the reindeer using every bit of cover the tundra has to offer. It does not work. The animals get increasingly nervous and break into a run—reindeer style, which is fast. I feel sorry for Karl. This is a bad situation that requires quick shooting. And while the herd is gaining speed rushing by us, I see Karl on his knees and hear his gun go off.

I know he is a crack shot, but we see no animal go down. Better safe than sorry. I grab my gun and see a reindeer cow slowing down, obviously unable to keep up with the herd.

Looking through the scope makes things clear. The right front leg is shattered. This is a bad situation that calls for a fast shot. I am the guide and hate to see an animal suffer or even get away with such a wound. Automatically, my hand cocks the Krieghoff drilling. I center the crosshairs and touch the trigger.

The 7mm bullet finds its mark, but the reindeer is still on the feet. Adrenaline does that.

I hand the gun over to my son when Karl's rifle booms again, and I see the reindeer cow getting knocked down.

Hunt over!

The herd disappears over the next ridge, and now we are all smiles. Karl breaks off a small branch from a bush and puts it into the reindeer's mouth—the last bite, an old German hunting tradition. We shake hands on a successful hunt, and then it is picture time. Karl is happy.

Rain, sleet, cold, wind, wet feet, hunger, dirty gear, miles of walking and climbing, disappointment—none of these things count any more. I reckon he realizes that he is blessed to be able to hunt in a foreign country and in an area as spectacular as the Hardanger Vidda.

He might never see this place again, but he will never forget it.

A trophy is not just measured in inches and points but also in the way it was taken. We know that this hunt will never be forgotten. This day will always be in Karl's mind.

Back to reality. After you squeeze the trigger, the work starts.

Karl, a butcher by trade, skillfully field dresses the deer. Two miles can be a long way.

After some serious dragging and hauling, we can see the road, then we can see our car, and finally, the reindeer finds a resting place in the back of Karl's station wagon. We are not cold any more. We are soaked.

Now we have to find Ola Garen, the postmaster, mayor, and policeman. He usually buys the meat. We have about 700 German Marks coming, which we need for gas. We also have to pay for the ferry to get back to the Island of Askoy where my parents-in-law live.

There, we want to spend a few more days deep sea fishing.

Ola Garen never lets me down. Meat as well as money changes hands.

"See you next year, Ola," we say, and we are on the road, reaching Askoy with the last ferry.

We have white wine, shrimps, and good company in my uncle's cabin. And let's not forget, I have my son with me!

What more could you want?

Date	:	May 19, 1992
Location	:	Eel River, New Brunswick, Canada
Hunters	:	Dale and Brian Craig
		Willibald Scheiter
		Olliver Kretschmann
		Mike Engster

I am an early riser, and long before 6:00 a.m., I am standing on the little pier at the Eel River. Fog floats over the water like white smoke. It is totally quiet.

The camp behind me is still asleep, so the first moments of the new day are all mine. One more time, I am on a hunting trip, and I think of countless hours of action and adventure that I have been allowed to experience due to this passion.

The first hunting license, the first doe permit, was back in Nattheim, Germany. The first reindeer was in Norway's glacier area, called Hardanger Joekulen. Brasil, Alaska, Kansas, the White Mountains of New Hampshire, the Carolinas and Canada—at this very moment, I have no idea that the best is yet to come.

My fellow hunters and guests are old friends from the Fatherland, which I left behind years ago to go and look for greener pastures. There is Willibald Scheiter from the Bavarian Forrest and Olliver Kretschmann, a friend of my older son Stephan. We are hunting for spring bear, and after the few sightings we had yesterday, I guess our chances are not bad at all.

Willi and Olliver saw some grouse and a big red fox, while I had a healthy looking black bear sow with two cubs right under my flimsy tree stand. Needless to say, no shots were fired except for those taken with the camera.

Behind me, up on a little ridge, sits our camp, consisting of three log cabins, a kitchen building, and a supply shed. I can hear someone handling pots and pans. I smell coffee, which is BS because I am too far away.

It is fairly cold down here at the river. I shiver and walk back to our cabin to wake Willi and Olliver.

Soon after that, I really smell coffee. We are sitting at a breakfast table with eggs over easy, bacon, bread and hash browns.

"Do you want some pancakes with maple syrup?"

Who could say no to such an offer?

A while later, we load our fishing gear into the big, green freight canoe, fill up the tank for the outboard motor, and then we are gone. The river is like an old friend. I know every inch of it—every turn, the beaver house, the eagle nest, the deep fishing holes, and the shallow spots where you do not want to wreck your boat. I remember one place in particular where I caught my first bass in Canada. This time, we are able to land a 3-pounder, but after this good start, things slow down. However, that does not keep us from enjoying nature, which still seems untouched, untamed, rough, and strictly grand. We see a lot of ducks. We see eagles. A moose crashes through the willows, and a beaver seems to be on an important mission. Needless to say, we are talking BLACK BEAR.

It is about 11 o'clock when we pull the canoe ashore, clean our fish (we caught four), and put them into the freezer. It's not much, but at least we caught something. There is still coffee on the old stove, and we have a cup. We do have another three hours to kill before we go out again to look for *Ursus americanus*—the bear. Then Dale, our Canadian guide and friend of previous hunts, drives into camp with his beat up, old pickup truck. It is two o'clock sharp.

A while later, Brian, his brother, stops his Toyota in front of the utility shed. They had checked out the bait stations in the morning and have a good idea where we might have some bear action in the evening. Now we are sitting over the map of the area, steaming coffee cups in our hands, and we discuss possible "hot spots" for bear.

Okay. This is the deal. Olliver will go to Page's Corner, Willi will be sitting in a tree overlooking the Eel River close to camp, and I will drive all the way to a place called Irish Settlement. Besides Willi, we all have a long way to go.

We wish each other "hunter's luck," shake hands, and are on our way. About one hour later, Brian's four-wheel drive pickup has reached its limits. I jump out, get my gear, say goodbye to Brian, and disappear into the Canadian bush.

The woods are swampy, and a lot of fallen trees make it hard to move fast. It takes me a while to get to my stand. The flies must have been waiting for me, and when I finally see a white plastic bottle filled with molasses tied to a tree, these little bastards have been sucking some of my blood already.

I climb up to my stand, which is about 10 feet off the ground. This is not a lot considering that bears are good climbers. A narrow wooden board is nailed between two strong branches, and that is where I will be sitting for the next few hours. This situation differs a lot from a good old German tree stand, which offers you serious comfort compared to this flimsy set up.

After one hour, your butt hurts—then your back, then your shoulders, then your legs—and when your whole body finally goes numb, the hordes of bloodsucking flies seem to pester you even more. You start to move some muscles and move your behind on the narrow seat just to find out that there is no comfort, and finally, you just give in to the torture. Hunting is supposed to be fun. This, here, is serious dedication!

6:00 p.m. Some squirrels chase each other through the trees. I hear small birds and the wind moving through the pine trees. I also hear the flies buzzing around my head, which is covered with a net to keep the little vampires away from me. 7:00 p.m. The same scenario.

8:00 p.m. The flies are still here, fighting the net. Once in a while, they get lucky. I do not count the stings any more but the cramps in my left leg. I shift my weight to get some relief while it gets darker. I look through the scope and put the crosshairs on the white plastic jug. There is still enough light for a clean shot. However, the scope on my single shot 30/30 Contender is cheap, and I start to regret that I gave my other guns to Willi and Olliver. Too late. The 30/30 has to do.

And then there is a dark shadow, silent like always. I have never heard a bear before I actually saw it.

Bears seem to be gliding through the woods. My heartbeat increases at once. Adrenaline shoots into my system. Hunting fever! My hurting back suddenly hurts no more, and the flies do not bite me any longer. Tension. Anticipation. Adventure. The human being turns into a predator. The rest of the world does not count any more. Total focus!

Fifteen and then twenty minutes pass. Nothing moves. I can feel with every fiber that the bear is still close. Here he is again. I have an eight foot wide trail. That is my shooting alley, and when the bear crosses this trail, his body length covers the whole width of it.

The sow I saw yesterday was half the size of this monster. I cannot shoot. Everything happens too fast, and there is just not enough time left to digest the situation. The head of the big bear shows up again for a second and disappears. No shot possible. This bear knows that something is not quite right. Another 15 minutes of nothing. Then the same game starts all over. There is no chance to shoot, and it is getting darker and darker. I should actually leave my stand and walk out of here back to the four-wheel drive, but I just cannot do it.

9:15 p.m. Here he comes again, using all the cover available. I raise my gun in slow motion, pull the hammer back, and try to put the crosshairs at the target. I can hardly see anything, just different shade of dark grey and black. I cannot risk a shot.

"Keep your cool," I tell myself, and that is when the bear gets up on his hind legs, trying to get to the sweet stuff in the white plastic can. I put the crosshairs on the only semi-white spot, and when the body of the bear covers it up, I squeeze the trigger.

The distance is about 35 yards—too short to hear the bullet hit. The bear makes a bellowing sound and crashes through the underbrush. One more time, there is nothing else but silence—if you do not count my heartbeat.

The tension of the one-and-a-half hours slowly fades away to be replaced by nervousness. I have to check the spot where the bear was shot I have to find blood, I have to find his tracks, and I have to find the animal before it is pitch dark. And, right here, lies the problem!

It is far from smart to follow a wounded bear, especially such a big one in the darkness with a little, single shot rifle. At least, that is what I tell my students when I teach the hunter education classes, and now I am standing in the darkness, all by myself, looking for blood and having a hard time seeing things that are more than five yards away.

And, by the way, there might be a big, angry bear in the brush close by! The situation starts to make me increasingly nervous. I hear all kinds of noises. I have to get out of here. There are too many dark shadows. The bear could be right beside me, and I would not even realize it. I do not feel like the great white hunter any more. I feel like a big fool.

I made too many basic mistakes tonight because I got carried away like a greenhorn.

But then again—shit—nobody is perfect.

The way back to the four-wheeler is long. It is more stumbling through the night than walking. Brian, who is nervously waiting for me, gives me a look which is like a question.

"I took a shot. Maybe it was a little too dark, but I have a good feeling. I think I hit him hard."

Brian is a good guy and does not give me a hard time. "We will find him tomorrow. I am glad you are here, and now let us get out of here."

We are creeping through a rocky riverbed and along some bumpy logging roads towards our camp. I am sure Brian knows

My biggest black bear ever!

exactly how I feel, and I am thankful that he does not talk about it. We will see tomorrow.

I try to remember every detail and start to feel better. It was a good shot—high on the shoulder, but good. Whether the 30/30 caliber was big enough to do the trick, however, remains to be seen. Always use enough gun! I might have broken this rule tonight.

Olliver and Willi have been picked up by Dale. They are sitting in the main lodge, steaming coffee cups in their hands and the big question on their faces.

I fall into a chair, and we exchange stories. Willi saw a coyote, but he had not wanted to spoil his bear hunt by shooting a little "wolf". Our Canadian buddies see this completely differently. They would have shot. Olliver watched a fox and, later, a porcupine. His gun also stayed silent.

Before we finally hit our bunks to be ready for the early morning "search for the bear" mission, I think I have told my story at least half a dozen times.

I do not know if my friends have a good sleep, but I toss and turn. In my dreams, I see bears chasing me.

Needless to say, we get up early. The regular, slow breakfast routine goes overboard. We are in a hurry, which actually does not make a lot of sense. The bear is either dead or gone.

One more time, Brian has the chance to show us what his 4x4 truck is able to do while he tries to get as close as possible to the "crime scene." Eventually, he stalls the motor. The poor vehicle has been pushed to the limit.

One more time, we work our way through the Canadian brush, rifles ready. Do not bring a handgun! The Canadian game wardens would not like that.

And then we are there. I think about what happened last night and try to find a blood trail, but the howling of my friends tells me that this is not necessary. Here he is!

Not even 20 yards away, a monster black bear lies halfway hidden under a fallen pine tree. We shake hands. They pat my back over and over again and wish me, "Waidmannsheil", which means "hunter's luck" in German.

I must have a wide grin on my face. I placed a good shot. We did not have to search for a wounded animal, and I bagged a trophy of a lifetime. On top of that, I am together with friends. They are happy for me, and looking at them makes my throat tight. These are the things that make a hunting trip into something special that will never be forgotten. It does not get any better.

Photo session. We try to catch this moment. We snap a lot of pictures, and then the work starts.

Yard after yard, hour after hour. This bear is heavy. The brush is thick, and we are soaked in sweat when we finally see the truck. It is done. The time is high noon. Back at our camp on the Eel River, a bunch of people are waiting for us. More photos. The scales show 425 pounds, and that is field dressed. This is a bear for the Boone & Crockett Book. I am happy, to say the least.

That evening we celebrate, and German and Canadian hunting stories are told—some of them true and some of them not so true. Our Canadian friends even start singing, and when we finally run out of beer, we have friends for life. We might also have a hangover come tomorrow morning. But today is today and tomorrow is far away.

You want to know how the rest of our trip went? Well, Olliver had no luck, but Willi was able to shoot a nice black bear two days later while I was busy filling the freezer with trout and smallmouth bass. The time was flying. The days at the Eel River were too short. My friends had to go back to the Fatherland, and I had to go back to the US. The daily grind was waiting for us all, but we brought back stories and memories, and our batteries were charged again. This will not be our last hunt. We will meet again. I am sure of that.

Reflections 1

Sitting in a tree stand or in a blind waiting in vain for whatever game might be called a waste of time for most people. I see this with different eyes. I am close to nature, my senses are alert, I am listening to the little sounds of nature that cannot be heard in front of a TV, a computer, in traffic or with a cell phone glued to your ear. You have time to also focus on the small animals out there. Birds, squirrels and even mice.

Sometimes your mind drifts off and you remember things of your past like being a first grader in 1952 going to the Bruchsal Elementary School located in the City garden on top of a hill called Belvedere about 3 kilometers away from our house. There was no school bus so I had to walk to school, rain , shine or snow.

I was a skinny kid. Timid shy and very poor. And I was always afraid to get into a fight with Bertold the class bully. Our teacher was Mr. Joseph Mehl, a tall and very strict person who everybody was afraid of. He was not shy when it came to giving his students a serious spanking but I liked him for whatever reason and I will never forget his sad eyes. He might have experienced bad things during WW 2

One day we went on a field trip, needless to say on foot. We had a little picknick and played some games. Eventually Mr.Mehl paired us boys up for wrestling matches. Eventually I heard my name. "Michael, it is you and Bertold." It could not have been worse.

Bertold was looking at the girls and then he was looking at me. I was not an opponent for him at all.

Afterwards I felt sorry for him because he had no chance of winning this wrestling match. I tried to hurt him and I did. I was not shy any more, I was not the poorest kid in the class any more, I was not the kid that had no father any more.

Finally Mr. Mehl stopped the fight. "It is o.k Michael." That was all that he said and from that day on the class of 1952 looked at me in a different way and from that day on I hardly ever lost a fight and I definitely could not be bullied any more.

May be Mr.Mehl did this on purpose, maybe he wanted to take my fear away. I never found out. He died shortly after but I did not forget this man.

In 2015 I visited Germany and showed my wife my old school that I had not seen for 63 years. The big tree where our first grade picture was taken still stands and I still see Mr.Mehl standing there waiting for us in the morning.

Date   : Fall 2002
Location : Somewhere in Georgia
Hunters : Tom, Ben, and Rodney Bryant
            Art??
            Mike Engster

The cold cabin starts to wake up. The snoring that kept me awake half the night stops while Ben tries to get the heater going. Later, he tells me why the place where I hunted from yesterday is called "the crying stand." Too many people had missed too many deer at that particular spot. Well, I had missed nothing last evening, but I had not seen anything either.

After a quick cup of coffee, Ben, who seems to be the ramrod here, decides to bring me to a different location.

Another cup of Ben's black brew, then everybody wishes everybody good luck, and one by one, we disappear into the woods.

Ben leads me to a long and narrow field. It is still pitch black outside, and we have to use a flashlight to get to my spot. Ben wishes me good luck one more time. Then I am alone, which is what I like anyway. There is something about darkness, nature, and being all by yourself. It clears your mind and lets you think. You go back and see yourself as a kid with torn clothes, an empty stomach, and big eyes watching the US soldiers in an occupied Germany. You see yourself going to school and later joining the military. You see mistakes made and opportunities missed. You question the course of your life and your "accomplishments." You wonder how other people might think of you, something that never bothered me too much.

And then you think about all the places where you went hunting, and you have a hard time counting them all—the adventures, the people you met, the deep satisfaction of a successful bear stalk, the nights at a camp fire, howling wolves and grunting moose. The list goes on.

I shake my head and go back to the present. About 300 yards

south of me, there seems to be some action. Through the binoculars, 23 wild turkeys take shape. The first sun rays find their way through the trees as I watch these interesting birds for the next 20 minutes before they slowly wander into the brush.

It is now 8:45 a.m. No deer! Something urges me to follow the turkeys. Sitting tight has never been my strength, so I walk slowly to where the turkeys disappeared. I put the binoculars on my eyes and look through the trees until the head of an 8-point whitetail buck seems to pop up right in front of me.

I am standing in the middle of the field without any cover whatsoever. The buck looks straight at me and stomps the ground with his front leg. This is not really the perfect situation.

From now on, everything happens in slow motion—if you do not count my heartbeat. I put the binos down and ease the Blaser rifle from my left shoulder into my hands, always looking at the buck. My right thumb pushes the cocking lever forward, and the gun goes very slowly up against my shoulder. The buck gets nervous. I squeeze the trigger as soon as the crosshairs line up with the buck's chest, and the deer does a back flip. 180 grains of metal can do a good job, and my heartbeat goes halfway back to normal. The rest is routine. The deer gets its last bite (an old German hunting tradition) before my knife goes to work to do the field dressing. I am plain happy to be alive on this day at this place.

The next "tool" is my pocket camera, and then I walk back to the camp to get one of the four-wheelers. Later, my deer is loaded up. Driving back to the camp, I meet Ben and Art. Art is a guy I do not like who shoots a 45/70 Springfield Trapdoor rifle. They are not happy. They killed a small, 4-point yearling with several shots out of the Springfield, and trust me, there is not a lot of usable meat left.

The real problem, however, lies in the fact that the man already killed a buck and shot this one supposedly by mistake. It fits the picture, and I keep my mouth shut. I am a guest here.

I have no doubts that they know exactly what I am thinking. Ben does not look pleased either. He is a great guy and handles the situation as tactfully as possible. After my buck is tied to the meat pole and we take some pictures, the whole crew meets at the breakfast table where eggs, onions, bacon, corn muffins, potatoes and coffee are waiting for us. Ben and Rodney Bryant are camp cooks de luxe! We talk about the events of the morning. We saw deer but no shootable bucks except for the one that I bagged. But we are not done yet.

The afternoon is filled with work. I butcher my deer and put the meat in a big cooler. Rodney, who will take the meat home, takes care of the ice part. He is handicapped and cannot move around too well, and I cannot take the venison all the way back to Oklahoma anyway. Rodney is a good guy and definitely likes the idea of having a freezer full of meat for his family. I continue my camp chores and boil the deer head to get it ready for a European mount. It is time consuming work that keeps me busy while the rest of the crew takes a nap.

Later in the afternoon after the camp wakes up to more activity, Ben gives me directions to a nice pond.

After sighting in a few guns, a chore that, in my book, should be done before you go hunting, I take the four-wheeler and head for the pond, a beautiful spot that is overlooked by a mansion. It must be nice to be rich.

I take it easy, catch a few bass, and try to drive back to camp. I say try because I end up in a ditch and flip the vehicle over. It lands on top of me, but only my pride gets hurt. Back in camp, I totally forget to talk about it.

Nobody has shot anything. They had the misses and the wrong deer, and I think the guys do not want to further screw up in front of a stranger.

We have deer steak, bread, and beer for supper. It is good like always. We talk about hunting, guns, knives, women, the military and politics.

At 9:30 p.m., the lights get turned off. I had a good day. I feel a little lonely and do not know why, but deep inside, I am Okay.

In the middle of the night, I have to go outside and nearly step on a coyote sneaking around the camp. For a moment, this guy scares the hell out of me. The sky is clear and full of stars. The air is cold and fresh. The wind from the north rustles the dry leaves while someone inside the cabin snores like hell. I am getting cold and rush back to my sleeping bag. My thoughts go in all kinds of directions before I drift into sleep again. There is something about a camp that touches your soul. I cannot explain this. You either feel it or you don't.

Date   :   April 8, 2003
Location: Osage County, Oklahoma
Hunters :   Tom Bryant
            Mike Engster

My wife, Sonja, wakes me up early. I have to be at the hospital at 7:45 a.m. for another test after a very unexpected cancer surgery. What else is new?

They fill my bladder with some sort of fluid, put me in another one of their big machines, and take all kinds of pictures. Nothing really hurts too badly. However, the whole procedure is just plain uncomfortable.

A doctor shows up, tells me that things are healing well, pulls out my beloved catheter, and tells me that I can get dressed again—but not without feeling this really sharp pain in my private parts.

Well, all the tubes and probes have finally been removed from my body, and hopefully, this is the way back to normal. But now I have to wear diapers. What a great feeling that is. Sonja brings me back home. I do not feel like talking.

Later, I make some business related telephone calls. I want to go back to work. Thank God my sons take care of things. And so I try to be a good patient and hope that I am not too much of a pain in the butt for Sonja, who has been very understanding and helpful during the last few weeks. I guess I owe her.

In the afternoon, I read hunting magazines and see myself roaming the woods. I have to get back in shape. Supper is ready, and getting out of my bed, I wet my pants. I clench my fists and grind my teeth, feeling helpless one more time. This is a humbling experience to say the least. After cleaning myself up, I go back to bed. My dog has the same idea, and we both take a nap.

Later in the evening, I call my neighbor. Sonja does not hear me.

I get up at 5:30 in the morning. Looking down, I see a big, red scar and a belly that is strangely out of shape. I do not feel good about what I see and ask myself if my life will ever go back to normal.

I put new diapers on (for the last time), get dressed in hunting gear, grab my shotgun, put on my boots—which hurts—and silently leave the house where Tom Bryant is waiting for me already. Slowly, I climb into his truck, and we drive off to Charlie Creek where we do the hoot owl call to stir up the roosting turkeys. There is no gobbling to be heard. The big birds do not respond.

"Let's go to the Donelson Ranch and try our luck there."

Driving east on Highway 60, I try to ignore the pain in my abdomen and concentrate on turkey hunting. The sky in the east turns from dark grey to a bluish steel color with a pink rim on top. South of Elmond Fox's big wheat field, we get out of the truck to do the owl call again.

The turkeys answer immediately. The adrenaline level goes up, the pain is gone, and the hunt is on. We sneak up to a big, round bale of hay and sit down in front of it.

Tom gets his turkey caller ready and starts talking turkey.

Within minutes, we see five gobblers. It does not get any better. It is still fairly dark. We see only shadows. But my gun is up, and I am ready.

The minutes pass. The sky gets brighter. More turkeys leave the roost and fly north, which is away from us, and land in the wheat field.

Tom tries to call them in. They respond by gobbling but keep heading away from us. We have to be more aggressive, at least that is what I think, and so we move a little closer using all cover available. We hunker down behind some big trees and watch the flock of turkeys out on the field, still out of shotgun range. And that is when a big tom gobbler turns around and walks straight at us followed by three jakes.

Slowly, my gun comes up, and the turkey stops. While we are focused on its strutting performance, the younger turkeys get out of the field and into the trees.

Tom keeps his turkey music going, which at least fools the younger birds, and while my friend is not in the position to shoot, I ease my Benelli up to my shoulder. Still, I cannot get a clean shot. There are too many bushes between us and the birds, and they get more and more nervous.

"Shoot," whispers Tom, but I still have to wait.

One of the turkeys turns and starts walking away. Big mistake. I see his head exposed and pull the trigger. Feathers fly. The bird flops several times. Tom shakes my hand, and Mike is happy. I bagged a turkey while I should have stayed in bed. I see the new, green colors of spring changing the country. I feel the sun. I have good company. I can ignore the pain in my belly and the thoughts about cancer and just feel good. Yes, I feel good for the first time in quite a while.

Tom picks up the bird. I unload my gun and watch the rest of the turkeys running across the wheat field. We go back to our car. This was a good morning. This was better medication than pain pills, and Sonja's breakfast is rich and tasty.

"Do not pull another stunt like that," she says while we pretend not to hear her, shoveling food in our faces.

Yes, by gosh, it was a good day!

Date   :   October 5, 2004
Location :   Little Sandy Creek, Wyoming
Hunters :   Harry King and Liz King
             Stephan Engster
             Mike Engster

For the last two days, we have been hunting in the mountains north of Sandy Creek without any success, not an elk in sight.

As non-resident hunters, we are not allowed to go into the so-called Wilderness Area, but that is going to change today. Liz King, who is a Wyoming resident, accompanies Stephan and me, so we are legal to go further up the mountains.

Her father, Harry, a real nice old gentleman, is also tagging along. Going northwest, it takes us about 1.5 hours to work our way up to the Wilderness boundary.

Please note that my son, Stephan, has a cast on his leg, wrapped in plastic and tape. How he gets along with this thing beats the hell out of me. I guess he is just a tough guy.

We take a break up on a ridge overlooking the valley of Little Sandy Creek and Sheet Lake.

To the east of us lies the Continental Divide. We glass the area for a while, but we cannot detect any elk. We decide to split up and go different directions to cover a greater area, look for elk sign, and just get a better idea of this place.

Liz and her dad want to go straight north along the ridge. Stephan goes southeast while I work my way down towards the Little Sandy.

All by myself, I become part of the woods. I love to "still hunt" and take my time to get down into the valley. Sometimes I sit for half an hour glassing before I move to another spot with a good view. The landscape is breathtaking. However, I do not see anything but three mule deer, does, some crows and some squirrels.

Time flies, and when you are all by yourself in a setting like this, your mind starts to wander. You lose track of time. I have to meet Harry and Liz at 6:00 p.m. up on the ridge, and it is 5:00 p.m. already.

I look at the mountain in front of me and wonder how to climb this thing in one hour. I throw my pack and my rifle on my back and start my way uphill, and that is when I let my guard down! My rifle is on my shoulder with my pack. I start to fumble, and at the same time, I watch three cows and a 4x4 elk disappear into a thicket not even 50 yards away from me. There is nothing I can do. The situation is strictly f— up, and what could have been a good opportunity is gone.

I have 55 minutes to get up to the ridge of this mountain, and being Mike Engster, I do not intend to let Harry and Liz wait, wondering where I might be. Straight up I go. No time to look for trails. My pack and my gun get heavier. My canteen is close to empty. Off and on, I stop for a moment to get my bearings straight. I am sweating profusely and get more and more lightheaded.

I have 15 minutes left to get to the top, and I make it. My knees buckle, but I try to look good meeting Harry and his daughter two minutes past 6 o'clock. I feel really sick. Harry gives me water and some dried fruit and shakes his head. He is a smart person.

"Why?" he asks.

"Because I said so," I reply, and we leave it at that.

Liz and Harry were hunting the ridge, but their luck was as good as mine. We start our descent towards the camp and hear an elk cow calling. Harry gets all excited, but then I see Stephan sitting under a big pine tree working his elk caller.

Darkness sets in, and we walk back to our camp in silence. We watch some grouse and two beaver about 300 yards northeast of our camp. The moonlight reflects on the water, and the whole setting is just beautiful.

Stephan and I are the camp cooks for tonight, and our deer stew gets very good grades.

We share a little drink, some camp talk, and hunting stories from the good old days. We enjoy the nightly coyote howling serenade and then the cozy warmth of a sleeping bag. The night turns out to be scary. I have hot flashes. My heart flutters with my heart rate fluctuating from 70 to 200 beats per minute. Soaked in cold sweat, I wait for this to stop. I do not dare to move. My eyes are wide open, and when the morning light creeps over the mountain tops, my situation starts getting better. I am just glad to be alone.

The colors of the fall surround me when I step out of our tent. I have reached the fall of my life and wonder what will be coming my way. The long scar on my belly hurts. Chemotherapy or radiation treatment might be waiting for me, and right now, I do not feel like a man anymore. I am just a thing!

During the rest of our trip we do not see any elk except a dead one, killed by one of our camp guys, and then our time is up. Good times always pass too fast. Now the stress of our techno world is calling out for us again.

During the last evening, we share a drink and a lot of true and not so true hunting stories with comrades. We have eight people here in this camp, people with completely different backgrounds, different education, different age and different political views, and the only word that comes to my mind describing this evening is HARMONY. There is a bond between us that only a hunter can feel.

Date   :   March 11th 2005
Location: Omunjerrke Farm, Namibia
Hunters :   Martin Engster
            Michael Fechter, farmer and PH
            Sonja and Michael Engster
            Trude Olsen
            Bernhard, Foreman of Omunjerrke Farm

We slept good during our first night in Africa. Now at about 6.30 in the morning the birds, and they have more then 600 species in Namibia, do a great job waking us up. Rolli and Balthasar assist them telling us it's high time to get up.

Breakfast is served in the main house and we find everything from smoked Hartebeest, Oryx liver sausage, Zebra biltong, wild honey, marmalade made of cactus and much more on the table. Ideas about diet or losing weight go right out of the window. We are joined by Michael Fechter, his two kids, Katrin and discuss the plans for today while the black maids, especially Elizabeth ask us in perfect German if we need more coffee. We feel like at home. Everybody is friendly and relaxed.

Sonja and Katrin have to drive to the airport to pick up Trude, Sonja's niece from Norway while Michael Fechter, Martin and myself want to go on a little scouting tour and sight the rifles in which will happen a little different as planned. And so we climb on the little Mitsubishi safari truck and put our guns, a Blaser combo 9.3x74R — 16 gage and Martin's Adamy double in .470 N.E. in the gun racks. We will find out soon enough that you can not have enough gun in Africa even when you hunt "only" plains game. Our driver is Bernhard from the Herero tribe, a big guy who is also the foreman of the Omunjerrke Farm. He handles the truck well but has a distorted relationship with the clutch, however he has eyes like an eagle and stops ever so often to show us different kinds of wildlife.

The nature and landscape is breathtaking and we have to restrain us from taking too many pictures. Rolling hills, dry river beds, rock formations, brush, tall acazias, lush green valleys and dry open plains — it is all here and we are in the middle of it. I look at my son who has been tested to the max by personal tragedy. He looks back at me and smiles. Getting closer to a windmill Fechter asks Bernhard to stop. A windmill indicates a waterhole and we want to make a little stalk. There is a bunch of Oryx in front of us and there might be a shootable bull among them. The hunt is on !

We jump-of the tuck and get the guns ready. Following Michael we try to sneak up to the waterhole just to find out that you do not sneak up to a herd of Oryx on every given day. They spot us and are gone. One the far side of the waterhole Fechter makes us climb a big tree stand after he made sure there are no tree snakes or hornets. We have a great view but see no wildlife other then birds. This scenario however is about to change. The old Oryx bull is limping through the camel thorn brush heading for the waterhole, his right hind leg dragging.

"Looks like he has been wounded in a fight", Michael whispers. "I think you should take him before he becomes leopard food."

I get my gun ready and cock the action. The Oryx, totally unaware of us being here slowly approaches the waterhole. " Usually we don't do this, but this one is hurt. Giving him to the leopards would be wasting good meat."

I nod in agreement and put the crosshair. s slightly behind the shoulder of the bull. Shooting at a slight forward angle this should be just perfect. I push the double set trigger, take another breath, halfway exhale and the 286 grain round nose soft point bullet hits with a thud.

Nothing happens, the Oryx just stands there. I have a 16 gage rifled slug in the upper barrel of my gun ready to go. Fechter understands the question in my eyes and whispers: "He is dead, don't shoot again. He is dead, he just does not know it yet ."

30 seconds — nothing, 45 seconds — nothing, then the legs start to wobble ever so slightly and finally the great antelope collapses. "I told you," Mike says.

We are shaking hands, unload the guns and get off the treestand. Walking up to a downed animal is a big part of a hunt, at least for me. We do this very careful, an Oryx can fight off lions with his 3 feet rapier like horns and he can definitely hurt a careless hunter in a heartbeat. So when we walk up to this great African animal my gun is loaded again . The beast is dead — long live the beast!

We shake hands and take pictures while Bernhard is pulling up with the truck. We find a gaping wound on the right hindquarter of the Oryx. We made the right decision and we are going to have Oryx steak tonight while Fechters farm workers will have their share of the meat. I will have a great trophy on top of all this.

Bernhard gets the cooler and we are breaking out the beer before we load this big animal up to head back to the farm. It is 10.45 a.m. and I am happy !

With the help of a little winch we pull our prey onto the truck, secure the head of the Oryx and start rumbling towards Omunjerrke not knowing that more action is waiting for us right over the next ridge.

And that's when Fechter knocks at the rear window and Bernhard stops the truck. "There are some good Kudus in this brush over there and we should probably take a closer look." This is invitation enough and we are off the truck. This time it is Martin's turn and he slips two cigar sized .470 cartridges into his double rifle. My gun stays on the Mitsubishi, however I am armed with a camera and my binoculars.

Michael quickly spots the biggest Kudu and the hunt is on. We sneak through tall grass and thorny brush just to loose the

big bull. Watching the wind as good as possible we approach a patch of trees and I see the Kudu again. Now we have reached the adrenalin stage. Deep crouch and we take another look to find out that the bull vanished again. How you can loose such a big animal within a few seconds beats me. We look at each other and Martin shrugs his shoulders. At least we tried, and that's when Michael Fechter grabs Martin's arm and points at two horn tips sticking out of the brush.

We see the bull but Martin can not get a clear shot. The Kudu cannot see us and slowly moves to the left entering a tiny clearing. Martin puts his gun on Michael's shooting stick , and when the Kudu steps into the open the big double rifle roars. The bull jumps, turns around on his hind legs, stumbles and goes down. A second 500 grain bullet makes sure that the hunt is over. What a day: Two good trophies in less than two hours. Waidmannsheil Martin and congratulations on some nice shooting!

The Kudu is strictly beautiful and will live in our memories forever. This was hunting the way it should be. Stalking always gives me the greatest thrill and here we are in Africa surrounded by nothing else but nature ,with our hearts full of joy and thankfulness for being alive today and for being blessed to experience all this.

While we are busy taking pictures Bernhard pulls up with our safari truck and after another beer we have a hard time wrestling the Kudu on top of the Oryx. The Mitsubishi will have a hard time hauling us through the bush back to the farm.

Eventually we are there after having been bounced around for the longest time and unload our animals at the so called butcher barn where two farm workers armed with big knives and hatchets are already waiting for us.

We are tired and sweaty, take a shower, have a serious gin-tonic and relax at the pool where Sonja and Trude are already getting the African sunburn. A lazy afternoon at the pool surrounded by numerous birds, small talk, a little drink under the grass roof, a nap and nothing else but relaxation.

At about 4 o'clock in the afternoon we grab our guns again and head out for a little evening hunt. Sonja and myself get dropped off at a big tree stand overlooking the dry riverbed of the White Nossob on one side and a waterhole on the other, Michael Fechter , Martin and Trude go on a baboon stalk.

We see a lot of animals, mostly Hartebeest and Kudu, watch a Warthog with two little piglets and a bunch of noisy guinea fowl, red legged Frankolins and an abundance of smaller birds. Time just flies , and then we see our safari truck bouncing through the brush to pick us up with a big old and very dead baboon riding on the tailgate. Martin was lucky to end his life with three rounds out of Fechter's Bruenner CZ .223 rifle. Back in camp we get cleaned up and meet under the grass roof for a sundowner followed by a serious grill party with Kudu steaks and other good stuff. Katrin is a great cook and our second evening in Africa is full of friendship.

When we finally go to bed I have forgotten the world out there. My heart is nearly bursting; one of the best days in my life just came to an end and I was allowed to share it with my wife and my son. It does not get any better.

Date   : March 15th 2005
Location: Omunjereke Farm, Namibia
Hunters : Martin Engster
              Michael Fechter, farmer and PH
              Sonja Engster and Mike Engster
              Bernhard
              Hubertus

Sitting at the breakfast table at Omunjereke is always a good start to the day. However, I have no idea that this day will turn out to be very special for me. But let's not get ahead of the story.

We had had some great days already, and I have to mention that my son Martin shot a greater kudu after a very interesting stalk.

Hubertus, a retired game warden from Germany, Bernhard, the Herero driver, Michael Fechter, Sonja, and I mount our hunting vehicle and start bouncing along dirt roads and nearly invisible trails. We are not even a mile away from the farm when Bernhard hits the brakes.

Two jackals try to get away from us, but they are young and stupid enough to stop. While I try to snap a picture, Fechter urges Martin to shoot.

"They carry rabies, and I do not want them too close to my cattle," says Fechter.

Martin takes a quick shot with the .223 bolt action rifle, and I get the chance to take my photo from up close. Deep inside, I am happy that the second jackal gets away. Off and on, Bernhard stops the truck to give us time to enjoy the wildlife that he always seems to spot first. This, here, is the real thing and not the Outdoor Channel on our TV.

Another stop. We pull out binoculars and scan the landscape. Fifteen kudus, four bulls among them. One of them good and old. The hunt is on. The wind is not really in our favor, but there is no time to lose. With the rest of the crew

A happy moment with Bernhard, Sonja and Michael Fechter

watching us from an elevated point, the two Michaels stalk their hearts out.

At first, we cannot get close enough for a shot. Too many eyes are watching us, and too many noses check the wind. The kudus lead us on a wild goose chase. We can always see them but getting closer seems to be impossible. Today they are just smarter than we are. After stumbling through another dry riverbed we quit and head back to the truck, soaking wet—only to find out that the whole bunch of kudus just passed the trail about 50 yards from there. Go figure. We see more kudus on a slope along the other side of the valley. They look big to me but small to Michael Fechter. He is the PH. He knows how to judge them, so we keep on searching.

Our valley widens, with the grass along the riverbed growing tall between the trees. There are red and yellow flowers that cover the meadows like rugs. A warthog and some piglets cross the trail. A small herd of reddish-brown hartebeest head for thicker brush, and noisy guineas scatter in front of our vehicle. And that is when Bernhard steps on the brakes again. I have a good feeling when I finally see some spiraled horns sticking out of the brush. I remember Robert Ruark: A kudu is special. There is something about this lovely beast that makes him the hunter's grail. Perhaps it is the sweep of those double-curling horns—as brown and clean as rubbed mahogany, heavily ridged from the base around the curls, and ending in polished ivory points. Perhaps it is the chevron on his nose or his clean, gray, white-barred hide, the skin thin as parchment. Perhaps it is the delicacy of his long-legged deer's body, the slimness of his long deer's legs, the heavily-maned swell of his neck, the enormity of his ears that pick up whispers at a radar range, and its unpredictable escape routes.

Enough of Robert Ruark.

Fechter looks at me, "Six of them and one is very old. Are you ready for action?"

I grab my combo gun, jump off the truck, and check the loads, and one more time, the stalk begins. We have to go downhill first, through tall grass, and then uphill again. We lose sight of the kudus as soon as we get into the bottom of the valley. Our friends, however, can look into the hillside and see the whole hunt unfold. They have a balcony seat while we are struggling not to lose our bearings and get out of the tall grass and into the camelthorn brush.

Sweat stains my shirt one more time, but the adrenaline is flowing. My heart beats the hunter's way. These are the moments when basic instinct takes over and the predator deep inside of us comes to the surface. We do not feel the thorns scratching us. We do not care about the stifling heat. We are stalking our prey— alert, focused and ready.

There are six animals somewhere in the thicket in front of us, and we cannot spook them. We have to spot them before they see us, but we have only four eyes and they have twelve.

There is some movement ahead. There are horn tips, but they are the wrong ones. Where is the old kudu? Ever so slowly, we move to the right.

Fechter signals me to stop, "About 50 yards this way. Get ready."

Hell, I am ready. I push the cocking lever on my Blaser gun forward slowly and watch the spiraled horns of the old bull move to the left. A few more steps and I might get a shot. Michael Fechter has his shooting sticks ready. I place my rifle on them, taking a deep breath. My finger touches the trigger. The kudu steps further to the left. I apply pressure to the trigger, and a 9.3x74R caliber bullet finds its mark while the bull is angling away from us. The kudu makes a small jump and continues walking.

"He is dead. He just does not know it yet."

I open the gun and replace the empty shell with a new one, and when the kudu stops for a second, I wallop him again. Game over. Another few steps and he goes down.

We look at each other, and the two Michaels shake hands before we walk over to a very old and very dead kudu bull.

"One more year and this gentleman might have been leopard food after all. Good shooting, by the way."

The kudu is all that I have ever wanted since I read Robert Ruark's book *The Horn of the Hunter*. The horns are massive with the tips looking forward. The body is heavy, and even in death, this animal looks beautiful. As of now, it will be immortal for me. This day will be in my memory forever.

Michael Fechter looks at the teeth of the bull that show a lot of wear. "I am glad we got this one," he says while our Mitsubishi truck driven by Bernhard pushes its way through the brush towards us.

Congratulations are in order. I am grinning as I shake hands. Martin gives me a bear hug, and I feel like I'm on the top of the world with a feeling inside that I am unable to describe.

A photo session comes next before Fechter breaks out the beer. Hubertus—an ex-game warden from Germany, Martin—an United States Marine, Sonja—a housewife from Norway, Bernhard—a Herero tribesman from Africa, Fechter—a German-Namibian farmer, and I—an ex-German Navy guy from Oklahoma—drink together in the middle of nowhere. . For a short period of time things like politics, religion, or the color of the skin do not matter anymore. We are all the same—united by our passion, united by hunting. Think about that for a moment!

Date   : Summer 2008
Location: South African Union
Hunters : Martin Engster
           Ruth Reeves
           Jeff Smith PH
           Mike Engster

Hunt for Number Six of the Big Five.

The hippo is a large, mostly plant-eating African mammal inhabiting rivers and large lakes in groups of 5 to 30 animals. It is recognizable for its barrel shaped torso, enormous mouth and teeth, hairless body, stubby legs and tremendous size. It is the largest mammal by weight (1.5 to 2 tons plus) behind the rhino and the elephant. Despite its stocky shape and short legs, it can easily outrun an Olympic sprinter! The hippo is also one of the most aggressive creatures on the planet and is often regarded as one of the most ferocious animals of Africa. It is claimed that this species kills more people than any other animal except the mosquito. Steve Irwin, the Crocodile Hunter, considered a five minute sequence crossing a river filled with hippos to be the most dangerous thing ever filmed. Needless to say, we read all of this after we came back from Africa.

"Shooting a rogue hippo in the water is just hippo killing—not hippo hunting." These are more or less the words of Mark Sullivan, who is probably one of the most controversial hunters of our time. I agree with his statement up to a certain point, but I had no idea that my son, Martin, and I would have to live up to this statement first hand. After a four hour car ride back and forth to the town of Louis Trichard, we were unpleasantly surprised by an obese black official who denied us the hippo license that had been promised to us by the very same person. This is also a part of the "New Africa"—not everything goes as planned to say the very least.

Well, now we are sitting together with our PH Jeff Smith discussing our options. The whole trip has not really been a success so far, and frustration sets in. Some of our stuff was stolen, the food is lousy, my zebra hide does not have a head on it any longer, our luggage came four days after our arrival in Johannesburg, and the gun permits are missing. And like I already mentioned—we do not have a hippo license.

And so we retreat to the bar to have a stiff gin and tonic.

The whole day is shot, and the evening drags on with Jeff Smith out of sight. We are sitting here, close to the border of Zimbabwe, waiting to go back to the US. My son, Martin, and Ruth, his fiancée of two days, retreat to their cabin while I try to find Jeff.

He is on the porch, just putting his cell phone down. "I might have found a hippo. It is a five hour ride one way. If you want to go, talk to your son, and let me know what he thinks. I have to call this guy back ASAP."

"Call him now. We are going!"

So we leave our camp at 4:00 a.m. Jeff, Ruth, Martin, and I are driving to a farm called Waterberg where, due to lack of water, the hippos had a hard time and decided to be nasty and check out the fields and gardens as well as a newly established golf course and a new lodge. Civilization was closing in on wildlife, and one more time, wildlife was going to lose the battle. How do you teach a hungry hippo to stay off the GREEN of a golf course?

I look at my son. "If we have to be the executioners, let us make the best of it."

When we finally reach the Waterberg farm, a man with a .38 caliber revolver strapped to his hip welcomes us and leads us to a nice porch where we are served cold drinks. We are also told to keep our guns out of sight.

"We have a lot of animal loving guests here, and we do not want to upset them."

In my book, this is BS in its finest form, but what the heck.

He continues to give us instructions before we finally leave the compound, and the tourists behind us and head for the hills.

It takes less than 5 minutes, and we are back in Africa!

There are no more telephone poles, cabins, cars, roads, or people, but there is very rough terrain and an abundance of wildlife. A lot of pictures are taken: kudus, zebras, nyalas, warthogs, hartebeest, oryx, springbock and more.

We, reach an elevated place, get out of our Land Rover and walk up to a cliff overlooking a deep ravine and a small creek that feeds a little lake further down the hill. Glassing for hippo reveals nothing but a more or less dry river bed with some small leftover pools of water.

Our host explains, "This is the result of a long dry spell. We need rain, and we need it bad. The hippos are strictly starving, and that is why they act up like they do. They are just plain desperate and mean."

We continue going uphill on a bumpy track that seems to shake our teeth loose before we stop again. I feel sorry for Ruth. This is her engagement vacation, and we torture her like this. However, the best is yet to come!

The guy with the little revolver decides to check out the neighborhood for a particular hippo bull, and we start walking single file along what was once a river. Jeff, the PH, does not carry a gun. I am armed with a video camera like Ruth—only Martin carries his Krieghoff double rifle...without permission to shoot!

The going is rough with rocks everywhere, and while we are concentrating on not losing our footing, we come up to a little pool of water too small to hide a hippo. WRONG!

Just imagine you are in a swimming pool and holding a rubber ball under water, and then you let it go. Well that is the situation with a hippo bull popping out of this little, overgrown waterhole, charging us instantly!

Everybody is running uphill. Ruth stumbles and falls twice, and we have to help her up. Everybody is shouting and scrambling until the hippo stops and starts ambling downhill into the

It does not get any better!

thick brush. We are too excited to have felt any fear—the whole thing just happened too fast and came too unexpectedly. The fact, however, was that we were lucky the hippo did not like to run uphill on such rocky ground. We were also lucky to get a good look at that animal, which was all scarred and way too thin for a healthy hippo. In other words, we saw the one that had to go!

The battle plan is very simple: Drive downhill in our Rover to the small lake, make sure to get there before the hippo gets there, move upstream on foot to intercept our prey, and finish the job the right way. Let's do it!

It takes about another 45 minutes on rough roads to reach the water at the bottom of the hill. This time, our PH does not leave his gun behind. Now he carries a Heym double rifle chambered in .416 Rigby while Martin uses his trusted Krieghoff Big Five in .470 Nitro Express—heavy medication, to say the least.

Jeff Smith leads the way followed by Martin, myself, Ruth, and the guy with the small revolver. Slowly, we work our way upstream. The little valley is narrow, and the heat is getting to me. Very soon, my shirt clings to my body. I am soaked, and so are the rest of us. Every time the little creek makes a bend, we move around it with utmost concentration. Slowly but surely, our adrenaline level rises. Every step brings us closer to the kill zone, and then we see it!

The hippo bull has left the creek bed and is resting in a small patch of grass about eighty yards to our right.

"Let's kill him," says Jeff to my son. "If something goes wrong, climb a tree." He looks at me and grins. The biggest tree around is smaller than my arm. "Come on, Martin. Everybody else, stay back."

And then they move in while I keep the camera rolling. I do not think you can surprise a hippo bull in the open. Four thousand plus pounds of meat jump up. Martin fires the first shot, hitting the hippo straight in the shoulder. The bull does not even flinch, but he changes direction, now coming straight at us.

Just checking out some monstrous teeth!

Martin's gun goes off again, and the 500 grain solid hits the face of the attacking giant and knocks him down for a fraction of a second. The bull recovers in a heartbeat and continues his charge. However, he is slightly off course. It seems like the bull is aiming for the guy to my left, the one with the little revolver.

My son fires two more quick shots, and we see the hippo crashing down the riverbank. Now we all start running, but this time we are not running away. The hippo is still alive, and our PH asks Martin to shoot one more time for safety.

Remember, it is the dead ones that kill you!

And then it is all over, and we stand in front of an animal bigger than I have ever hunted before. It is hard to describe my emotions, but strangely, there is also some sadness in the mix.

In my book, one thing is for sure: Whoever came up with the term "BIG FIVE" definitely never hunted hippo on dry land—or forgot about it. This is the real thing. No kidding!

It's picture time. There's shaking of hands, big smiles, hugging, and more pictures after a bunch of black guys show up to butcher the beast.

Hunting has united us all—at least for the moment. Race, profession, religion, politics—at this very moment the world is at peace, and we are all brothers and sisters.

Tomorrow, when we get to the airport, things will be different again.

We hand the hippo over to the black guys. They will have a feast tonight, in the camp and cooking fires will be high.

We will not be there. We will miss out on the last chapter of this hunt, but we are pressed for time and have to drive back to our main camp close to Musina. Tomorrow, the long journey back to Oklahoma and Texas begins. Then we are not hunters any more but engineers, doctors, accountants, or whatever.

But when you leave Africa, it is said that you leave a part of your soul behind, so you have to come back to claim it.

At least, that is what they say.

On our way back to our camp, I realize that we experienced a hunting day of a lifetime. We might never do something like that again.

And then Mark Sullivan's words come back to my mind and put today's events into perspective: Hippo hunting is not for the timid. It requires great amounts of intestinal fortitude and plenty of good old-fashioned guts. Anyone can shoot a bull hippo form the safety of a river bank as he breaks the surface of the water to take a breath of air.

But that is not hippo hunting. That is hippo murdering, nothing more. On the other hand, I consider my kind of hunting the greatest "Bang for the Buck" in all of Africa. It is when you willingly lay your life on the line and enter the field in pursuit of the nastiest 13 feet and 6000 pounds of unleashed fury on the face of the Earth more commonly known as Mr. Rogue Bull Hippo.

But if you are not equipped with watermelon-sized testicles, you cannot play because your body, more specifically your mind, will not allow you to participate.

Your brain will tell you to walk forward, but your feet will not move. And no amount of coaxing and telling yourself that everything is OK will change any of that. Your feet will seem immovable, as if planted in two yards of cement, and that is before you ever find your first bull.

Time seemingly stands still. You know beyond a reasonable doubt that you are trespassing onto someone else's turf, and he might not approve. So far Mr. Sullivan's take on hippo hunting, this is what I have to say: I think that man is right!

Date   :   July – August 2008
Location :   Kalahari Desert / Namibia
Hunters :   Walter Milbich
                   Michael Fechter
                   Martin and Michael Engster

It has been a great trip so far, and it started out fast and furious with me shooting the oldest oryx cow possible for the slaughterhouse in Windhoek. I should have kept the horns. Trust me—they were long. The gun that I used was my trusted 9.3x74R double rifle.

Trying to show our friend Walter Milbich a little bit of Namibia, we left Omunjereke to go to the Kalahari Anib Lodge close to Marienthal. And what a place that was—a beautiful oasis in the desert with top notch accommodations, good food and most of all an abundance of wildlife. My son, Martin, had his sights set on a blue wildebeest, and after he showed the local guide how a Krieghoff Big Five in .470N.E. is used, nobody doubted his shooting skills any longer. He drilled a hole through the target, and I mean dead center.

Later that day, after a tricky but successful approach, Martin shot the biggest Wildebeest I have ever seen. It went down like it was poleaxed, got up again, ran about 50 yards, and crashed. A 500 grain bullet, well placed, usually does the trick.

We left the Anib lodge the next day to go to my favorite place—Nababis—where our guest, Walter, shot a gold medal Springbuck using a CZ bolt action rifle. The scratched up, one eyed, warthog that had obviously survived a leopard attack, fell prey to Martin's .470. The next day belonged to me. I had never shot a black wildebeest, and that is what we were after.

Michael Fechter told us over and over that you can hardly ever bring any wildebeest down with one shot without the animal getting up again. I bet against it and decide to leave my 9.3 rifle back at the farm and use Martin's Big Five for a change.

Hunting the Kalahari

As I will soon find out, this decision is right and wrong at the same time. We cover a lot of ground in Michael Fechter's 4x4 Mitsubishi before he, who else, spots a bunch of springboks with two wildebeest in their midst.

"They are both good. Let us go after them. We might have a little walking to do," he says.

I look through my binoculars and wonder how Fechter is able to see that these are two good bulls. I only see two black spots that are bigger than the brown spots around them. I guess our friend and PH is just good. He knows what he is doing, so we follow our fearless leader. The value of a trophy stands in direct relationship to the effort you put in to obtain the trophy.

We never get close enough for a shot. There are too many eyes out there. We cross a bunch of little creeks. We crawl through brush. We walk over the next ridge and through the next valley, and I wonder how we will ever find our way back to the truck. Further, I realize that Martins gun weighs a lot, and that is for sure and for certain.

Next time I will bring my gun along.

And by the way, it is hot today. We are drenched in sweat while the wildebeest and their companions lead us further and further away from our car.

But Fetcher says, "Stalking black wildebeest out here in this fairly open country calls for a lot of patience and a lot of sweat and walking. This is the Kalahari. This is Africa at its best. This is hunting and not just shooting."

Well, to make a long story short, we just cannot get close enough to take a shot with a .470 N.E. double and are about to quit.

The springboks, with the two wildebeest in their midst, stop in the middle of a wide, empty, brown meadow without any kind of cover. There is no way of getting closer and staying undetected.

We stop behind the last possible bit of cover and watch. We are about 350 yards away, and right now I miss my .300 Win Mag Ruger #1 rifle which would enable me to take a shot.

But then Michael Fechter says, "Listen, guys. This is what we do. We go single file and stay close. This is an old trick, and it might just work."

We do not know what might be so tricky about walking straight up to a bunch of nervous antelopes in plain sight.

Fechter can read the unspoken question in our eyes. "It is the oryx trick, just watch," he says and unfolds his shooting sticks to a big V and holds them over his head. "Let's go!"

It is a very direct approach, and amazingly, the animals do not run off but just look at us with their heads up. I cannot believe it. Then Fechter tells me to get ready and puts his shooting sticks down. I quickly line my gun up and send a 500 grain bullet on the way. The distance is about 130 yards with the black wildebeest facing us at a slight angle.

The shot feels good, but there is no reaction whatsoever. It looks like I have missed.

The springboks are in full flight while the wildebeest slowly turn around and amble down into a small valley just to show up again running uphill on the other side.

"It was a good shot, I know it." It is easy for me to say that because one of the wildebeest has stopped on wobbly legs and then drops like a ragdoll.

It does not take long to get to the downed animal that turns out to be a black wildebeest in the gold medal class that was hit straight through the chest with the bullet traveling through the length of its body. We find the projectile right under the skin of the right hindquarter. These animals are tough, to say the very least.

One more time, Michael Fechter and his guiding skills came through. I only had to do the finishing touch with a well placed shot. My friends shake my hands, and I am in the middle of the photos that are taken.

Our PH breaks out a bottle with warm gin that tastes incredibly good. Everybody talks. We are happy. We had a great stalk. We had good company. We hunted the Kalahari. We are the only people out here. Africa belongs to us. It does not get any better.

However, let us not forget that the work always starts after shots are fired, and when we finally, hours later, reach the farm with a wildebeest on our truck, we are more than pleased to see the trusted black farm workers who help us unload our prey.

They will be butchering tonight while we are allowed to be lazy and enjoy another one of these remarkable nights on a farm called Nababis with the campfire casting wild shadows, a star filled sky above us, and the voices of Africa around us. Then we finally go to bed and blow out the candles (Nababis is too remote to have electricity). We all had a little bit too much to drink. Suffice it to say, I sleep like a baby.

Hunting the German Roe Deer

Date   : August 2009
Location: Lauchheim, Germany
Hunters : Waldemar Kiener
           Michael Engster

The roe deer is for the German hunter what the whitetail deer is for the Americans. It is a much smaller deer, and a six point buck tipping the scales (field dressed) at forty pounds is considered respectable.

The hunting season lasts for about nine months, and the shooting of these animals is done in a very selective way.

Please note that the German hunter has to go through some rigorous schooling and pass a tough test—written and verbal—to get a hunting license. Needless to say, schooling is not free, and you might have to spend 1500 Euros or more before you take your gun to the woods.

In my younger days, while I was still living in Germany, I happened to be friends with one of the instructors now doing most of the shooting for the Natthein Forest & Game Department. I am in Germany on a business trip visiting my friend of 51 years, Waldemar Kiener. We went to school together. We hunted and fished together. We drank our first beer together, dated the same girls, and practically lived together until I had to join the German Navy.

Well, here we are sitting in Waldemars living room talking about hunting and where to go this afternoon. Then Waldemar fits me with some green clothes and the necessary hardware for the job on hand, and I end up with a Blaser R95 rifle in 30/60 fitted with a serious looking Zeiss scope.

We jump into the Mercedes 4x4 (Waldemar does not go cheap), drive to Lippach, the next little village, and talk to his hunting partner on this particular lease. One more cup of coffee and we head for the woods.

Roe Deer Buck about 2 years old

After a short ride through places I had not seen for many years, we park the car, get our gear and walk along the edge of a pine forest to our tree stands. Waldemar wishes me, "Waidmannsheil," and takes off. He will be sitting close to a clover field about half a click further west. Fox, deer, and Russian boar can be shot, and after I settle down on my ladder stand, the waiting game begins. From my spot, I see some fields, a small valley, a country road, and far away I can even see the monastery of Ellwangen. Unfortunately, I can also see a lot of traffic. Remember, we are in Germany, which is about the size of Texas. The population, however, is 80 million people!

I start thinking of the good old days that were not that good after all, me being the poorest kid in the village. My way out was the Navy, which provided me with opportunities and education and helped me to become what I am now.

What I am doing right now, however, is not so good. I am freezing. The German summer does not always provide you with warm temperatures. Cold wind from the west pushes dark clouds our way, and soon it starts to rain. There are still no deer in sight.

I guess the animals are smart and just stay at home.

I, for my part, leave my tree stand and seek shelter from the rain under the huge pine trees. By now, it is uncomfortably cold, and I hope that my friend feels the same. Then I spot something far away across the street on the other side of the valley.

Who cares about rain? This is a roe deer, and it is running full speed my way. Now it crosses the street, and through my binos I can see that it is a buck. I hurry back to my tree stand to get a better view, lean against the ladder to get a good rest for my rifle, and get ready.

After all of the years hunting all over the world, I still get buck fever. If that ever does not happen anymore, I promise that

I will quit hunting!

The buck is out there on the field, still running hard and not slowing down whatsoever, so I have to pull the old trick on him. Letting out a sharp whistle stops the roe deer in its tracks, and while the buck pricks up his ears and looks in my direction, I apply the necessary pressure to the trigger.

Through the powerful Zeiss scope, I can see every hair on the deer's body. 120 yards, an easy shot, and a 150 grain Winchester Power Point bullet is definitely heavy medication for an animal that size. Game over. I do not have to reload. The buck is down for good, and I forgot to mention, I do not feel cold any more. And so I walk over to the downed buck and put a little pine tree branch in his mouth. This is the last bite, an old German hunting tradition honoring the game you were allowed to hunt and to harvest. Silly? I do not think so. The world would definitely be a better place if people would do everything they do with a little more style and dignity.

Here comes Waldemar, who had had the same deer in his sights. Well this time I beat him to the draw. We shake hands, take some photos, and while Waldemar goes to get his Mercedes truck, I quickly field dress the deer. Remember, we want to get out of the rain. And then we drive back to Waldemar's house, through the countryside I grew up in. It feels good to be back here, and for the first time in many years, I wish that I would have never left. But then again, when I was young, I always had the urge to leave and see the world outside. I guess I have done that.

Back at the house, we put the deer in a big freezer while Hanne, Waldemar's wife, sets the table where we have great food. It gets washed down with the beer from the local brewery. Stories are told, and needless to say, the lights go out very late. We had a great day!

Tomorrow, I will leave Germany to go to Austria, Slovakia, and Hungary before returning to my home in Osage County Oklahoma.

Date   : March 2008
Location : Entre Rios Province – Argentina
Hunters : Martin Engster
                  Nestor
                  Jim Weber
                  Mike Engster

"Hi, Dad, we are going to Argentina!"

I do not know what my son is talking about, but while I was outside loading a few guns into my truck, some hunting trips were auctioned off during the SCi Banquet in Oklahoma City. Martin was lucky enough to buy a water buffalo hunt in the Argentinean province of Entre Rios.

We drink to that, and needless to say, we have a lot to talk about on our way back to Ponca City.

About seven months later, we, that is Martin, our friend Jim Weber and myself, go through customs in Buenos Aires, and I feel somehow naked traveling without my own gun.

I guess I should not have listened to our host Eduardo (Teddy) Fairhurst, who told us over and over not to bring any firearms.

"I have whatever you need and more on my farm," he said.

Well, we own Centerline Firearms, Inc. and are anxious to see Señor Eduardos arsenal, but first, we have to get out of Buenos Aires, which turns out to be quite an ordeal during the morning rush hour.

Finally, the city disappears behind us while we are crossing the Parana River. Eduardo proudly calls it the Amazon of Argentina. For the next two hours we drive through swampy flats with the horizon so far away that it stretches your eyes. Some shacks on stilts signal the presence of a few not-so-rich people, and we wonder what these swamp dwellers do to survive. Whoever turned the clock back turned it back quite a bit. This does not look like the 21st century.

Another road block! I wonder where all of these policemen come from and what they do in such a desolate area. I also wonder where the money comes from to pay all of these guys. They are everywhere! The free, democratic, liberal state of Argentina obviously does not offer too many liberties. That is, at least, what I think.

Eduardo stops at a rundown restaurant in the town of Qualequay where we eat fat and greasy beef. Thank God that we can wash it down with wine and beer. Our next stop is the town of Macia where we get gasoline, and after about 120 miles of soja bean fields to the right as well as to the left, on dirt roads that do not deserve to be called roads, we are finally at the Palm Tree Ranch. It turns out to be as run down as the restaurant in Qualequay.

The next day turns out to be quite uneventful, but at least we learn a little bit about the area. Two days later, we are out in the dense and moist brush looking for water buffalo. Martin was successful already, and now it is my turn to go after the big bovines. I carry an old BRNO bolt action rifle in .458 Win. Mag. with a scope as old and beat up as the gun. And YES, we should have brought our own hardware.

Our guide, Nestor, a full time gaucho, speaks as much English as we speak Spanish while our host and interpreter Eduardo remains on the farm. Therefore, the language barrier is obvious. And when our shirts finally cling to us, soaked with sweat, Nestor, our "pointman", motions us to stop. BUFFALOES!

Jim and Martin have to stay back while the final approach starts. Nestor and I duck walk for about 30 yards, and I finally see 5 water buffaloes slowly wandering away from us. I do not get a chance for a closer look when Nestor points at the buffalo to the far left and orders me to shoot. I do not see the horns and have to assume my guide made the right decision. I still hesitate to take the shot. I only see the buffalo's rear end, and nothing about this situation feels right.

The so called "Texas Heart Shot" is not exactly what you want to get out of a hunt, but Nestor urges me sternly to shoot. And that is what I do, against better judgment.

The buffaloes take off, and I mean all of them. And it takes only seconds before the dense, wet bush swallows them. Nestor, our gaucho guide, gets up and starts running through the brush. We follow him, not seeing anything.

Finally, completely out of breath, we reach a clearing. So far, there has been nothing else but more sweat and senseless running through the jungle. Our guide hears something, and with the guns ready, we approach a little knoll covered with brush and tall grass. Adrenaline de luxe. Here is our buff!

Well, I do not really want to talk about us stalking a regular COW, but this is what we are doing right now. That is enough! Martin and Jim Weber decide to have no part in this adventure any longer and just sit down, sucking on their water bottles.

I, in the meantime, try to remember some Spanish words like *sangre* (blood) and *perro* (dog), and finally I get my point across. We, that is Nestor and I, make our way back to where I shot at the buffalo and find a small blood trail that peters out after a few short yards.

We need help and finally get in touch with some farmhands thanks to the walkie-talkie that miraculously starts working again. It does not take long for two horsemen and some mangy looking dogs to show up, and after a short discussion, the canines are turned loose on the blood trail.

Not even 30 seconds later, the buffalo, which had run in a totally different direction then we had, is found and cornered. The dogs bark like crazy. The two horsemen take off while Nestor and I try to catch up running. And then we are there!

The scenario presents itself like this: Three dogs are inside a bunch of dense brush surrounded by a belt of grass at least six feet tall. Two riders on nervous horses circle the place while two breathless guys try to figure out what to do now.

A close call in the 1960s

Shooting is impossible. So the first thing is to get the riders out of the picture. After this is done—and it is not easy—I climb on a tree stump to get a better view. Finally, I manage to spot a piece of black hide, and with all the dogs being brown, I squeeze the trigger.

One way or the other, the buff has to come out of the thick stuff.

I have a hard time describing what I feel at this very moment, but I definitely miss my double rifle. I am on high alert. I am totally cool. I put another round into the chamber and crank the scope down to low power. I am ready. At least, that is what I think. But when the wall of grass in front of me suddenly breaks open, there is no time to raise the rifle to my shoulder. With the gun halfway up, the bullet is sent on its way.

Better lucky than good! A .458 Win. Mag. bullet can cause quite a lot of damage, and when a water buffalo is shot through the neck and its spine gets broken in the process, its frontal assault is stopped cold.

The last cartridge goes into the chamber—a safety precaution.

When the smoke clears, there is a distance of about six paces between me and the buff. This is when I realize that I put myself willingly in harm's way with a gun not really fitting the job.

I am not that cool any longer, and I feel my knees shake a little. I hope the gauchos don't notice it.

I have had some close encounters before in my life. This one, however, should not have happened.

Well, all is well that ends well, and when Martin and Jim, alerted by the gunfire, show up, we take the pictures that will give us the bragging rights back in the USA. Deep inside, however, I do feel good. This is not the buffalo I wanted, and I definitely did not like the way the whole hunt went down.

The gauchos use their horses to drag the buffalo into the open and start butchering the animal on the spot while the skinny dogs get their share in the process. We feel out of place and decide to walk back to the farm.

Martin, the Marine, leads the way but is replaced by Jim Weber (US Army). We have the feeling that we are going into the wrong direction, and so the German Navy takes over. Too late.

We are tired and hot and lost in the jungle and still too proud or too stupid to admit defeat. What a great day this is! Finally, I ask Jim for his lighter (thank God we have a smoker in our midst) and set a palm tree on fire. This is the standard procedure here, and it takes less than an hour for big Jose to show up on his pony. I have the feeling that the smirky grin on Jose's faces is also to be seen on the face of the horse.

Later in the evening, drinking red Argentinean wine and having a conversation with our host, Eduardo Fairhurst, we slowly start to feel better. Being together with my son Martin and a good friend like Jim Weber puts me at ease. It makes a not good day turn good. It fills your heart and makes you thankful for what you have. To hell with Fairhurst and his buffaloes. Life is good, and by the way, let's have another glass of wine.

Date   : July 2010
Location: Waterberg Area / Namibia
Hunters : Joerg
                   Michael Fechter
                   James Weber
                   Martin Engster
                   Mike Engster

We left Omunjereke early yesterday morning, and now we are in the middle of nowhere, or at least, that how it seems. The place is located in North-Eastern Namibia, and the 60,000 acre farm we are on is as old as the German history that surrounds this remote place. This is the place, by the way, where bloody battles were fought at the beginning of the 20th century between the German Protection Troops and the warriors of the Ovambo, Herero and Nama tribes. A lot of blood was spilled right here. This morning, I spilled some blood myself while hunting for warthog with Mr. Joerg, the owner of this farm and great grandson of the colonist and horse soldier who hacked a living out of this rough country. That colorful and tragic story is documented in the book *Lorang*.

This is my third week in Africa and my second day here, and I have seen more wildlife that you can shake a stick at. It does not take long before we see a major warthog making its way through the brush. Then Joerg asks me if I can hit it. I do not take this as a question but rather as the green light for a shot. Slowly, I reach for my Krieghoff Drilling, push the cocking lever forward, line up my sights and touch the trigger. One more time the 30/06 proves to be more than a warthog can digest, and the pig dies in its tracks.

Even without measuring the tusks, we know that this warthog is gold medal class, to say the least. Next, we take the bragging pictures before we get the beat-up, old truck, load up the hog, and drive back to the farm. I meet my son Martin there.

Family Time in Africa

Grandfather

Father and Son

He was lucky to shoot an oryx with a broken off horn. Meat for the freezer!

We are both spellbound by the breathtaking scenery and the abundance of wildlife and wonder what the evening might bring.

Joerg talks about an ongoing leopard problem which has resulted in 13 cows being killed within one month.

"What if we ever get to see a leopard?" I ask.

"Just shoot it. I got the permit," is Joerg's answer.

And when God likes to punish you, he listens to your prayers. I am going to find out that there is a lot of truth to this statement. But first we all take a nap.

Late in the afternoon, three pairs of hunters leave the farm. Martin and one of the black guys go for warthog and/or big oryx, and our friend James Weber is looking at I do not know what while Joerg and I try to find an old kudu bull.

Nobody really thinks of a big, stealthy, spotted cat.

And so we end up sitting in a ground blind close to a little pond and have a good conversation trying to figure out life in general. I take a lot of pictures of all kinds of wildlife and watch the sun go down.

One kudu bull sparks our interest, but with a horn length of an estimated 45 inches, this animal still has some growing to do.

I see a movement to my right, and so does Joerg.

"Leopard," he whispers while I nod and get my gun ready.

This is most likely a once in a lifetime opportunity, and I am as ready as a person can possibly be.

Even with the fading light, it is easy to find the cat in my scope. The leopard walks slowly towards the water, stops, scratches the ground with his hind legs, and marks his territory while I center the crosshairs of my Leupold scope in the middle of the cat's left front shoulder.

I set the trigger of my drilling. The sight picture is perfect. This is an eighty yard shot—an easy shot, a penalty kick, a piece of cake.

I am calm. The bullet hits the cat, which gets knocked over and rolls down the small bank before it hits the water of the pond.

Done deal! It does not get any better!

It does not get any worse either!

As soon as the leopard hits the water, the big tomcat comes to life again and runs into the brush to our left.

Everything happens so fast that there is no chance whatsoever for a second shot.

Silence.

What happened?

Well, we both saw what happened and shake hands. It is a cold evening, and it will be an even colder night. No worries. We will pick the cat up in the morning.

It is too dark by now.

And so we wait for James Weber and his driver to pick us up.

We are all excited, and back at the ranch, a little celebration is on order. The cattle killer has finally met the fate of all cattle killers, and I have to tell my story over and over.

This night, I sleep like a baby. I am happy and see a full body leopard mount above the fire place in my house in Oklahoma.

Life is good.

Mr. Joerg wakes me while it is still dark, and we head for the bush and the little pond where we park the four-wheel drive truck. By we, I mean Joerg, his tree hugging female partner from Chicago, Strubbel the poodle, Michael Fechter from the Omunjereke farm, James Weber, the black tracker and I. To be honest, I am a little bit surprised by this constellation.

James is ordered to stay on top of the truck to cover the back-trail. I show the black guy where everything happened last night. We find no blood, but we do find tracks. The "hunt" is on.

Joerg carries a shotgun. Fechter uses his Mauser 9.3x64. I have the drilling with the scope taken off. This is dense brush, and following a wounded leopard is probably one of the most dangerous situations in the first place.

Before the tracker really goes to work, I tell the crew what I think we are up against, "This was a good shot last night. I hit the leo on his left shoulder, and with a 30/06, there might not be an exit wound. That is why there is no blood. With a shot like that, animals might go another 50 to 100 yards before they expire. Everybody who has ever hunted whitetail deer knows that. So I think the cat should be over there, dead."

"We will see."

And so the black tracker follows the tracks for maybe 30 yards. Then he stops, scratches his head, and disappears into the thick brush. Everybody follows, and nobody likes to listen to my protest. Nobody wants to hear that the leopard ran to the left. I do not understand what's going on.

And so we follow what, in my book, are the wrong tracks while the poodle has a good time and the woman, completely unaware of the possible danger, acts like she is looking for mushrooms.

We do this for nearly one hour.

We find no trace of blood, and the tracker gets more and more uneasy. I look at my friend, Michael Fechter, who is not happy. Please note that Fechter is a long time African PH with a world of experience.

But we are guests here, and Mr. Joerg calls the shots. Further, Fechter's brother is married to Joerg's sister, which means nobody is going to rock the boat.

I am utterly disgusted and call the search off!

Everybody is happy about that but me and James, who has been sitting on the truck for quite a while.

We drive back to the farm in silence. There is "sand in the gearbox" to say the least. Eventually, I have to listen to all kinds of wild speculations, and when I finally meet up with my son Martin, I just want to leave this place, which is what we do an hour later. The farmer's girlfriend-wife stays hidden. No goodbyes from her, but what the heck—I did not like her in the first place.

And so we head for the Etoscha Pan where we stay for three days watching African wildlife and have a great and unforgettable time before we return to Omunjereke.

Back on the Fechter's farm, we do some incredible shooting, and then it is time to climb into the plane to leave the Black Continent for this time. But before we do that, Martin is lucky enough to bag a nice Caracal tom that could not resist the leopard bait we put out a while earlier. And so we do not leave without a cat after all.

Footnote: Two days before our departure, we receive a telephone call at Omunjereke. It is Mr. Joerg, and he apologizes for the unprofessional way the leopard situation was handled. He also invites us on a leopard hunt should we ever come back.

Life is full of strange surprises.

Reflections 2

Spring 1966

We just spent four long weeks in the cold North Atlantic chasing Russian submarines in bad weather. Now I know why this was called the "Cold War". Trust me, the North Atlantic is always cold and you are always wet and uncomfortable. At the time I was a crewmember of the German destroyer "Bayern " D183 responsible for all radar and sonar equipment longing for going ashore no matter where.

And it finally happened when our ship reached the Norwegian navy base Hakoonsvern where we were supposed to stay for about a week. The first day I had to stay on board —guard duty. And while two thirds of our crew went to the next big city Bergen I was walking up and down the pier with a rifle on my back.

The next day however, some of my buddies and I took a taxi going to Bergen looking for girls at the "Fregatten" dancing hall. The place did not disappoint. The dance floor was crowded, the music was good and the girls looked pretty, most of them blond.

After checking the place out it was time to make a move and the two girls at a small corner table caught my eye. A blonde and a brunette. I always liked brunettes better and so this girl was my target if you can call it that. One of our younger officers was two steps ahead of me and (what else) asked the brunette for a dance which she quickly accepted. And so I was stuck with the blonde whose name was Sonja.

We had a great evening, all of us sitting on the small table drinking Solo (a yellow lemonade) because no alcohol was served. I have to mention that we did not come totally unprepared and the yellow juice was spiced with good old German schnaps which we brought along. Sonja's girlfriend was called Ranveig which sound like " runway". We thought it to be a strange name.

Anyway, like mentioned before, we had a great evening and talked the girls into meeting us again the next day .

When things are good they usually do not last long and our stay in Hakoonsvern was cut short by some order from German Navy Headquarters. I had to say good bye to Sonja but promised to come back to Norway at Eastern I guess she did not believe a sailor.

Guess what — Easter (came and I was on the way north just to find out that she was visiting friends in Germany. You talk about being p... of.

Fate however plays a big role in human relationships and on a rainy day in Bergen I saw a woman with a blue suitcase and blue shoes hiding from the rain under a big umbrella coming my way. I recognized the shoes and stopped her. It was Sonja looking at me in disbelief. I was still mad and told her so in uncertain terms.

We had dinner in the evening together with her girlfriend Ranveig. I visited her parents on the island of Askoy the next day and was surprised by the way these people treated me. Why ? Sonja's dad was a prisoner of the Germans during WW2. Ole Olsen and I were friends from the first moment and I still get teary eyed when I talk about him and all the great days we spent in his fishing boat out on the fjord. And by the way —next year Sonja and I are married for 50 years. Not too bad !

P.S. We still are in contact with Ranveig Markussen who lives now in Denmark.

Date   : March 2006
Location : Nababis, Kalahari
Hunters : Michael Fechter and Katrin
                James Weber
                Martin Engster
                Mike Engster

Fechter wakes us up while it is still dark. We brush our teeth by candle light and have a quick breakfast out on the porch. At breakfast, we meet Fechter's brother, Horst, who is quite different from Michael. He does not strike me as a go-getter, and his farm, called "Falkenhof" which we saw on our way, looked kind of run down.

After a second cup of coffee, we push off into the bush. Some black wildebeest appear on a far off ridge. Blue ones, however, we do not see.

Jim Weber wants to go after his special friends, the baboons, and we drop him off. His plan is to stalk along the Packriemen River, going back to the farm. We wish him luck. He might need it. The baboons are very smart and cannot be approached easily. Sometimes I think they can tell if you are carrying a gun or not.

Well, Jim Weber is in pursuit of his monkeys while we are still trying to spot some blue wildebeest. Fechter (Who else?) detects a sizeable herd of black wildebeest with two blue ones in the middle. We are still far away, and I wonder how he can see these things. I guess he is just plain good at what he is doing. I respect this guy and his calm and friendly way.

He stops the truck. "Well, Mike, are you up for some serious belly crawling?"

Please note that this is not really a question but more like an order.

"Hell yes. I was born ready. Bring it on, buster." I am excited, and I am ready.

Martin stays back with the truck, and the sage colored brush swallows us. It is hotter than hell. My shirt is soaked in no time and clings to my body. I see nothing but brush, rocks, and thorns and try to keep up with Fechter, who obviously knows which direction to go.

We hit a small clearing, and looking around, I get my bearings back. From now on, we do the duck walk, and I feel like I'm in boot-camp again. Fechter drops to his knees. We can hear them before we can see them. The wildebeest must have noticed something—they are all lined up, looking in our direction. Then they start snorting and growling, kind of like dogs. Just think about it. You are sitting in the middle of nothing else but thorns and about 50 big, black beasts are growling at you. Awesome. Just, awesome. My heart races. This is all a hunter can ask for. This is an adrenaline rush at its finest. This is the real thing! This is the "poor man's buffalo" that we are after.

Two blue wildebeest slowly separate from the herd and move to our right. One of them is a very respectable, mature bull. We get into a super fast duck walk followed by a super fast regular walk, always trying to use all the cover available to us. Sweat is running down my back. Sweat is running into my eyes and makes them sting. My face is bathed in sweat, and sweaty hands hold the heavy cape gun. My luck, this is by far the hottest day so far.

The two bulls have stopped behind some heavy brush. They act nervous and might break into a run and be gone, and I do not have a clear shot. Fechter hands me his shooting stick. I am ready waiting for my chance. Both bulls are looking at us, one of them moves slightly to the left. I have the crosshairs of my scope centered on his chest, trying to find a hole in the brush to shoot through.

One more little step and my rifle kicks against my shoulder while the 286 grain bullet finds its mark. This is an eighty yard shot, brush or no brush, and I do not miss at eighty yards.

The wildebeest jumps up high, turns around, walks three or four steps, and goes down. Waidmannsheil!

Trust me. I do not care about the heat any more when Michael Fechter shakes my hand. I am a happy camper, 100 degrees Fahrenheit or not.

"Good shooting, old man. Let us walk up to him and take a closer look," says Michael.

And so I get to see the first blue wildebeest of my life up close. What an animal! I am standing in front of a magnificent bull and feel elated and somehow sad at the same time. This bull is dead, but he will be alive in my memory as a rugged and majestic animal as long as I live.

I look around and see miles and miles of grass and brush that looks as endless as the blue sky above us. I feel small, great, happy, and blue, and I wonder how many more of these moments God will grant me before my journey is over.

Fechter seems to feel what is going on inside of me. "If you ever have to get away from whatever you want to get away from, you can stay on Nababis as long as you want, and I mean for free."

I shake his hand, mumble a thank you, and walk away. My throat is tight.

In the meantime Martin has managed to get the truck through the brush and the rocks and boulders. Fechter signals him towards us, and like always, we have our photo session and a sip of warm gin. Martin looks the wildebeest over to find my shot that left no exit wound.

"Not too bad for an old man."

Hell, I feel young right now despite the fact that I have been called an old man twice within half an hour. Something is wrong here.

After a short discussion we decided that this animal is worth a shoulder mount. If you look at the picture you will know why. This is not a cape buffalo, but today that is what it is for me. The value of a trophy cannot always be measured in inches, points or pounds.

The spell this whole situation put on me slowly fades away and reality sets in. We have to get this animal out of the heat,

Blue Wildebeest – the poor man's buffalo

Packriemen River at the edge of the Kalahari

and so it gets loaded on our trusted little truck, which turns out to be another sauna session.

On the way back to Nababis, we try to locate Jim Weber. Doing so, we see some spectacular country along the Packriemen River. I might have to think about Fechter's offer to live here after all.

When we finally pick up the worn out baboon-hunter, we find out that Jim saw a lot of these monkeys without ever getting a shot at one of them. He still had a great time and enjoyed himself greatly. He, too, shakes my hand on a great blue wildebeest while Fechter does his "balls to the wall" cross-country four-wheeling with the poor truck. And while the wildebeest definitely feels nothing any more, our teeth are getting loose from bouncing over rough terrain in breathtaking "Fechter speed."

Close to Nababis, we pass the huts where the black farm workers live. They are all sitting around a fire—men, women, children and some scrawny looking dogs. To me it looks like they are having a good time. At least, they laugh a lot, and I envy them for the basic life they are living. Three of them jump on the fender of the truck and start butchering the wildebeest as soon as the vehicle comes to a stop at the farm. I have field dressed and butchered many game animals and watch these guys with professional interest.

They are good, and that's a fact. It does not take long before the wildebeest is just meat. I go back to the old farm house and take a shower with semi-warm water. By the way, there is no electricity here.

Later, I find myself sitting on the porch, enjoying this extremely remote and vast land where only a handful of people try to make a meager living.

From my elevated location above the Packriemen River I can see a sea of grass that stretches forever to meet a far away horizon. There are some reddish bluffs to my left overlooking the brownish waters of the river and the only tall, deep green

This is the right way to cross a river!

Last hunting day on Nababis

trees that grow along the banks. Patches of yellow flowers and purple and silver colored bushes as well as all shades of green and brown add to a painting that only nature is able to create. Further away, behind the river, the land rises slowly to a rolling prairie with dark thorn bushes growing in the ditches. The rest is grass and more grass with white tips moving in the wind underneath a blue sky specked with some white clouds drifting lazily in the warm breeze.

Looking down the hill, I see the gravesite of Hubertus Mehnert, which looks like a small chapel. I think I know why this pioneer never left this place for long.

And then there are the sounds of all the various birds, the soft wind in the trees, and the beating of your heart, and you feel totally alive and very small and insignificant at the same time.

Slowly, everybody comes to the porch, Katrin, Michael Fechter, James and Martin, and now we all listen to Fechter's monkey stories which are very interesting and sometimes strictly hilarious. I really like this guy, the way he handles himself, and the way he treats his hunting guests. I like our conversations when nobody else is around and he allows a small look into his soul.

After a small snack prepared by Katrin and the black kitchen girls, we all try to take a nap, which turns out to be more like another trip to the sauna. Remember, there is no electricity and no air conditioning. I guess, as of today, I do have a better understanding why the first white settlers in my home state of Oklahoma lived in dug-outs.

Lying on my bed, I feel the sweat pouring out of every single pore of my body. I am soaked, to say the least, and try not to think of the upcoming summer in Oklahoma.

We climb back on our hunting vehicle about 4:00 p.m. and drive through a huge area covered with silver colored brush. The big warthog that we spot a little late disappears before we can get a clear shot. Lucky "pumba."

At the edge of the Kalahari

Ready on the sticks

We come to another river crossing, but this time, the water looks to be deep. Fechter is nervous about getting stuck in the river. It would be a long walk back to the farm.

"Hey, Katrin, can you take your clothes off and walk through? I need to know how deep it is." Fechter must be joking.

"Sure thing, Michael," says Katrin, and she strips down to her underwear and wades through the river while all the men either sit in the truck or on the back of it.

And so we follow Katrin to the other side where she greets us with her big smile.

"That will cost you a drink or two tonight, gentlemen. I hope you did not take any pictures."

"We would never do a thing like that." Laughter.

Katrin climbs back on the truck, and the search for the springbok continues. Martin switches guns. A Sauer & Sohn bolt action rifle in 30/06 replaces his .470 N.E. double "boom stick", which is definitely too much gun for springbok. After a few very long shots that only scare our prey, Martin stops listening to Fechter about holding high, puts the crosshairs of the scope in the middle of his target, and we have a very dead animal. "Waidmannsheil," Martin, and so we are done shooting on Nababis. We load the little antelope up and drive back towards the farm.

The evening colors are warm, and we have Fechter stop the truck at various times to capture the moment on film. Before we get close to the farm, all the plains animals seem to be lined up to say good bye. We pass blessbucks, hartebeest, wildebeest, some kudus, warthogs, as well as a bunch of ostriches while the baboons in the trees "yell" at us.

What an evening! At Nababis, the blacks are all outside sitting around their cooking fires, laughing and talking while the women stir whatever is in the pots, and the dogs are chasing the kids or the other way around.

Two teenage boys get up as soon as they see us and jump on our truck. They want to butcher the springbok, but more so, they want whatever is inside like heart, liver, kidneys and so forth. They eat it all!

And so we unload and let them get at it.

Soon afterwards, we meet on the porch where one of the black women has a big fire going. Katrin and her girls prepare the food, which turns out to be great as always. How they cook like that on an open fire amazes me.

Later on, with candlelight and a dying fire setting the stage for stories and memories from the good old days, I feel totally content. I do not miss the abundance of "civilization" we have to face every day, and I do not miss all the entertainment we can have by just pushing a button, not realizing that this kills our soul, dulls our brain and steals our imagination. Here, in the middle of nowhere, I find peace.

After most of the wine is gone and only Martin and myself are left on the porch, we have a few father and son moments, priceless moments that allow us to let our guards down and be who we really are. Tomorrow we will drive back to the city with the crowded streets, the barbwire fences, the noise, the smell, the crime, the nice main road and the dirty, filthy slums. And, by the way, there are no gleaming campfires in the city. Tonight, however, the air is full of Africa, and we sit in the dark and talk.

Do what you love to do. Do it without apology or guilt. It is your life, it is your money, and it is your time.

You have earned the right.

Life is incredibly brief, the world we live in is very uncertain, and at the end of the day, the government will get most of your money.

Take charge of the time and the money you have.

Follow your dreams!

I read this somewhere and liked it.

Reflections 3

Two more days of deer season. I do not feel good, my heartbeat is out of synch and the damned pills obviously do not do the job. I realize one more time that the sand in my hourglass is mostly at the bottom. Well, getting old is not for sissies and whoever came up with the "golden years" stuff does not know what he was talking about.

My thoughts drift back to my childhood and the people whose presence might have affected my life. One of them was Friedrich Wilhelm See burger my grandfather and he was definitely different than the rest.

There was a small river behind our house and there he went every morning butt naked with a bar of soap and when his washing ritual was done he swam to the other side and back. Nothing special you might think but you do not know Friedrich Wilhelm: He did this summer and winter. Tough guy.

I saw a lot of scars on his body (I was six years at the time) and later found out that he was cut down by machine gun fire during WW 1 close to Verdun where millions of people died within a few square miles. So they dumped Friedrich in a mass grave but he was hard to kill. He probably moved and was pulled out of the ditch and brought to a hospital which he left nearly two years later. However he was in pain ever since. I always was kind of afraid of him due to his stern nature.

One day he had too much to drink which happened about 4 times per year. Obviously he must have suffered from a serious hangover the next morning.

Well. We lived in a small all catholic village and at that particular day there was a funeral. The gasket was carried all over the village followed by all the mourners as well as the priest and the altar boys. They more or less stopped at every street corner to sing and to pray before finally reaching the cemetery.

And so they stopped in front of our house making a lot of "noise". This must have annoyed my grandfather with his headache and he decided to stop that by reaching to his revolver on the nightstand.

He was a great shot and it was easy for him to shot one of the top hats off of one guys head. You have to imagine what happened next. He nearly went to jail for that but who wants to see a WWI hero in jail. However he was the talk of the town for quite a while.

Needless to say our village had to be ready for another Friedrich Wilhelm stunt which there were many. The next one however is the best I heard of and it all happened because of my mother.

One day she came home from school and sitting at the dinner table she would not eat hiding her hands under the table. This did not fly with my grandfather. My mother started crying and finally showed him her hands. Some fingers were bloody. "Who did this?" "My teacher".

You have to know that at the time it was very common to punish kids at school. That usually happened with a bamboo stick. You had to hold your hands out and there came the punishment. Some teachers were overdoing this. "It will not happen again", that was all Friedrich Wilhelm had to say and so he went to the school the next day and asked to speak with Mr. Holzmann (I changed the name) who he found in a classroom on the second floor. They started a friendly conversation and niy grandfather asked Mr.Holzman if the window could be opened. "It is a little sticky in here." When this was done Mr.Holzmann found himself outside the window while Friedrich Wilhelm held him on his jacket and told him in uncertain terms that, should he ever have to come back, he would then drop him.

My mother was never beaten again. Later I went to the same Elementary School and Mr. Holzmann's son was my teacher. I was never beaten neither.

But my grandfather was not always lucky. Sometime in 1943 he went to his favorite guesthouse (pub) named Graf Kuno in Bruchsal. There he let everybody know that the private from Austria, this he called Adolf Hitler, would -never win the war. He might have said more than just that because when he left the pub he was not seen again and all clear to find him were in vain. He was just gone.

We lived at the east side of town in a house that was owned by the Forest Department and Fish and Game.

When the war was over manly soldiers coming from the east stopped at this house asking for food. My grandmother always helped. One day there was another knock at the door and a 6foot three skeleton was standing outside. "What can I give you to eat? How can I help You?" And the skeleton (79 pounds) answered: "Just let me come in, I live here! " My grandfather was back home. When he left his pub 20 months earlier he was snatched by the GESTAPO and brought to the concentration camp in Dachau. Nobody cared about the Iron Cross he got during WW1

Like I said before: My grandfather was hard to kill. Today, so many years later I wish we would have been closer. Today, so many years later I would have been able to understand him better but we cannot turn the clock back. After my grandmother died he married again and his new wife wanted us (my mother and me) out of the house.

I was nine years at the time and my world was coming apart. I saw my grandfather one more time when I was 19 years old. He liked my uniform. I was in the Navy. We had a good conversation. I promised to see him again. He died a few days later

Namibia 2006

Diary of a Hunting Trip

Foreword

by Mike Mistelske

In this, his diary of a trip to Namibia, Chapter member captures many of the flavors of Africa. Michael's writing style — the touch of his German "accent"- makes for delightful reading, and the reader can easily see and feel and taste Michael's experience.

Michael's diary is presented in three parts, starting with "Part 1" in this issue. Thanks, Michael, for sharing this with us.

We have in America the Two-Hearted River tradition: taking your wounds to the wilderness for a cure, a conversation, a rest or whatever. And as in the Hemmingway story, if your wounds are not too bad, it works. But this is not Michigan, or Faulkner's Big Woods in Mississippi for that matter. This is Africa!

Namibia 2006 —

Diary of a Hunting Trip, Part 1

1-27-2006
Another bad week for my family. Well, we did not have a lot of good ones in the last three years, years filled with tragedy and hardship.

I am walking south, cross Charlie Creek behind my house and go up John Wayne Hill. From there I have a good look over most of our little ranch, and there is also the place for me to think and reflect.

I just brought my son Martin home. He had surgery again and I wonder if he ever gets over the accident that killed his to-be wife and ended his career in the United States Marine Corps. He is a tough guy but I have seen him hurt too often. He needs a break.

The two car accidents we had this week, both of them not being our fault, just add to the overall misery. A big Whitetail deer ran into my wife's brand new car causing severe damage, and while Martin was in surgery a fat, ignorant, white trash woman without insurance but with a cell-phone glued to her ear, rear ended me in the middle of Oklahoma City.

To hell with her and her cell-phone! Now I am sitting on my beloved hill and start thinking about our upcoming trip to Africa.

Hopefully Martin will be totally recovered by then to enjoy some serious hunting at the edge of the Kalahari Desert on a ranch called NABABIS. We have another five weeks to get him ready, but he recovers fast and should be o.k.

This time Sonja, my wife for nearly 40 years, is not coming with us. Lupus and a bad back do not allow her to travel that far. What can I say.

However we have two other people going to share a new African adventure with us: James Weber from Connecticut and Susanne Scheiter from the Bavarian Forrest in Germany.

Susanne is the daughter of an old friend from the Fatherland, and she is very dear to my heart. She likes Martin and his little son Max, however these feelings seem to be somehow one-sided.

I hope that some fire might be rekindled on this trip. At least the two of them will find out where they stand.

We will see. Matters of the heart can not be solved with the brain. Unfortunately!

My thoughts drift back to our last Africa trip and the great times we had. The bond between people just seems to be greater when you are out there, away from the concrete, the noise, the deadlines, the rush hours, the every-day rat race and the thousands of faceless people in a deafening jungle called "City". Another five weeks and we will see a bigger sky again, and hear the sounds of the Black Continent.

I get up, grab my gun, walk the rest of our property south to the oil well, then west to a small ravine, back north, down the hill to Charlie Creek and to our house. Six deer cross my way but nothing else. Anyway, I have been walking for two hours and feel better.

2-25-2006

A few more days and we are in Africa. Things at home however are not too good. Too much stress and pressure, too many doctor bills and ailments, and while Martin is recovering, Sonja is plagued with another Lupus attack. All this creates tension and the feeling that life in general sucks. I realize that my batteries have to be recharged so that days like this can be handled, and I want to thank my wife right here that she never tried to stop me when I had the feeling to follow one of my dreams. I wish she would be able to come along like last time.

Later, watching a documentary about a guy who lived with grizzly bears for thirteen years does not really improve my overall depressed mood but gives me to think.

What makes a person abandon our "civilized" world and choose raw nature instead? It must be more then just bare foolishness. Maybe nature is the place where man can find himself or more so his soul. Maybe this is the one and only escape out of a corrupt world that answers only to the money god, no matter what.

Well, the grizzly man Timothy Treadwell got finally killed, but what about the thirteen years of fulfillment that he was allowed to have?

I feel strangely drawn to this troubled young man who tried to find himself in the wilderness just like David Henry Thoreau, Ralph Waldo Emerson, Muir, White Owl, Everett Ruess, Robert Ruark and Christopher McCandless to just name a few. They all were highly intelligent. They all did not fit into our world of progress. For them progress meant destruction of what they cherished the most: Nature!

Do not get me wrong, I do not want to compare myself with these people, but deep inside I envy them for their courage to follow their hearts. But then again, maybe it was not courage but desperation to escape a world they just did not fit in. Only they know.

Well, I am at least in the position to leave my world for a few days and feel the Black Continent again. Soul food? Damned right you are! And I am going to inhale it. You can bet on that.

3-4-2006

In the meantime, after realizing that Susanne Scheiter will not be with us, we made it from Ponca City to Wichita and from there to Atlanta where we spent a night in a not-so-good motel. There we met James Weber who came in from Hartford.

The early morning ordeal at the airport, security line, ticket line, security line again due to our hunting rifles, line during boarding, etc. is behind us. Thanks one more time to Osama bin Laden who created this clusterf....

Now we are stacked like sardines in an airbus, the most uncomfortable airplane that I know. Sal Island lies behind us and seven more hours from now on we should touch down in Johannesburg —South African Union.

Four hours' lay-over, two more hours' flight to Windhoek, security again, and hopefully Michael Fechter from the Omunjereke Farm will be there to pick us up.

Well, he did pick us up in his 4x4 bus, and after a drive through a nice African scenery including a detour-a road washed out by heavy rain, we make a right turn and trade the dirt road for a trail that leads us to our final destination.

James, who has never been here before, gets his first impression of Namibian wildlife. He also gets excited about the abundance of wild game.

And then we are there! Katrin, the woman of the house, as well as Rolli and Balthasar, the dogs of the house, are in the driveway waiting for us. I see even more familiar faces like Bernhard, the Herero foreman, little Petrus who takes care of all the horses here at Omunjereke, Karoline and Elizabeth, the mother and daughter team in the kitchen. It feels good to be back. We are shown to our rooms, decorated with hides and trophies; and we are told to be at the grass-roofed but for a supper accompanied by a serious sundowner.

Finally, we made it to Omunjereke Farm. I'm worn out from the trip.

Saturday 7.30 p.m.
The wine finally does the trick. We go to bed early. I guess I am too tired to think about our first hunting day.

3-5-2006

The birds wake me up, and there are a lot of them. The yellow weaver birds alone have at least 25 nests in the tree right in front of my window. It is dawning, and I can watch the sun rise from my bed. How come it looks so different here? Everything just seems to have more color, be more intense, more basic and alive.

I hope that the pictures that I am taking can capture the moment.

After getting dressed in my hunting gear I walk across the yard towards the main building where the breakfast table is set. "Guten morgen, guten morgen". It is always kind of strange to me to be in Africa getting addressed in my home language, which is German.

Well, let us not forget that 100 years ago this place was called German Southwest Africa.

I wave good morning to the people in the yard, pet the dogs and go into the house. The breakfast table is set and looks as good as the last time I was here.

Kudu liver sausage, smoked hartebeest, springbuck roast, sliced eland meat, cheese, home made sausage, all kinds of vegetables, marmalade, coffee, milk and juice. What more do you want!

In other words we have a great breakfast and start to discuss the course of the day.

First we want to look for baboons along the river bed of the White Nossob and then just play it as it unfolds. James Weber is also interested in an oryx and maybe a warthog. I will tag along as the backup shooter.

We mount up. Bernhard is the driver, Martin and James are the first in line to shoot, while Michael Fechter and I sit on the back seat with binoculars ready.

Everything is green, the grass higher then ever; this does not look like arid land any more; hunting will be difficult. Fechter tells me that he has never seen so much rain in his lifetime, and back in Oklahoma we have not seen rain for seven months. But the scientists tell us that the climate is not changing. Bullsh...!

We see a bunch of baboons, but our small stalk comes too late. They must have seen us and are gone. A warthog crosses our trail and disappears in a ditch. We stumble through the tall and wet grass, fall into warthog dens, get dirty and scratched up and go back to our truck. What a start.

Bernhard starts driving and we rumble slowly through tall grass and wet thorny brush. Like always, we are amazed by the great number of animals. Kudu cows, hartebeest, the black and white faces of the oryx, elegant springbuck, guinea fowl, frankolins and birds, birds and more birds.

We take a lot of pictures, and that is when we see a good-sized warthog making its way through the brush. The wind is in our favor and four guys, three of them each with a gun and one of them with a shooting stick, jump off of the truck. The stalk is on; adrenalin is flowing for the first time on this trip.

"Whoever gets the shot gets to shoot", Fechter says, and he is the PH and boss here. Martin follows him, James stays more to the right while I cover the left flank with my 9,3x74R ready for action.

A few tense moments, and the hog comes back in sight. Martin has the best position, Fechter gets the shooting stick ready, and I hear the .470N.E. boom. No more ifs, ands or buts — the warthog dies on the spot shot through the head with a 500 grain soft-pointed bullet.

Waidmannsheil and time to shake hands and take pictures. Martin did a super shot with his double rifle. Smiles all over.

My son, Martin; first day warthog.

These are the better moments in life, and we celebrate with some stiff shots of good old gin.

Bernhard pulls up and we have a new passenger when we leave the scene of the "crime". The farm workers will have a feast tonight.

I look at the pig, its big teeth; and I watch the blood running down the tailgate. My thoughts however are somewhere else when Bernhard hits the brakes. I nearly fall off my little bench seat. "Oryx, and a good one!" Michael Fechter and Bernhard see things before we even think about them. 'Well James, you want to give it a try?" This is not really a question, and our James Weber does not have to be pushed.

Martin and I stay on the truck and see the hunt unfold. Using every possible cover Fechter and James make their way closer to the two oryx. One of them seems to get nervous, wanders into the brush and just disappears. The second one starts moving back and forth to finally makes up his mind and walks in the wrong direction. In other words, the oryx moves toward the hunters, not knowing that danger is waiting.

I have my binoculars on the animal when it gets knocked off its feet by a 150 grain .300 Win.mag bear claw bullet. James obviously knows how to shoot a gun.

Bernhard pushes the truck through the brush, and for the second time we do the Waidmannsheil thing, drink gin with the left hand (an old German hunting tradition), take pictures and shake hands on James Weber's first African animal.

Needless to say, we have a very happy hunter in our midst.

Our friend, James; oryx - his first African animal.

After loading the gemsbok (oryx) onto the truck there is little room left for us, and Bernhard is heading towards the farm. Like always he tortures the clutch of our truck, but that is the way he drives — Herero style.

On the way back we find a dead kudu bull with nice horns in a dry river bed. We can not determine the cause of death and blame a poisonous snake. The animal is bloated already and does not smell too good. The vultures will be eating well today.

Back at the farm the boys are already waiting butcher knives in hand, ready to go at it. And that they do. With their share of the meat and especially the innards of these animals, there will be a food-party going down tonight.

I get myself cleaned up and walk over to the main house where oryx meat, noodles, salad and pudding is waiting for us. A small glass of wine washes everything down.

Nap time comes next. Jet lag is still kicking our butts.

Bernhard, Martin and James Weber are one more time ready to kill a baboon, while Michael Fechter and I are meat hunting for the Windhoek slaughterhouse. And so we slowly make our way north along one of the many washed out ravines. The beauty of the landscape that surrounds us is only topped by the temperature that leaves not a dry spot on my body. In other words: My mouth is totally dned out while my shirt and even my pants are soaking wet. Eventually I am just following Fechter without paying any attention, and that is when I run into him.

"Do not shoot me; shoot that old bull over there if you can." I wipe the sweat off my eyes. "Sure thing master Fechter". My gun comes up against my shoulder, the crosshairs center on the chest of the oryx, a clean trigger break and the oryx disappears in the tall grass about 120 yards away from us.

I put my finger on the rear trigger while we are walking up to the downed animal but there is no need for another bullet. Needless to say, I feel good.

My old bull oryx.

We check the teeth and find them worn down to the gum line. "I told you that this is an old one. Good stuff for the sausage factory. Nice shot, by the way". Fechter does not say things like that too often.

Berhard must have heard the shot and comes crashing through the brush. One more time I am amazed what these farm vehicles have to go through.

We have a "Waidmannsheil Drink" and load up the second oryx of the day. Further hunting does not produce any additional meat, and we make our way back to Omunjereke to enjoy another African night under a grass-roofed but with steaks, potatoes, squash type stuff, salad, pudding and various sundowners.

We make plans for tomorrow to go to Auas for eland. Martin's big quest is to harvest one of these impressive animals. James is a fountain for jokes and so is Martin. We have a few good laughs before the lights go out.

3-6-2006

After breakfast we load our stuff into Fechter's hunting bus and drive to the Auas Game Lodge. We have been there before but that was a few years ago. Auas has been getting bigger catering mostly to tree huggers and animal watchers but it is still a very nice place with an abundance of wildlife.

I meet some familiar and some not-so-familiar faces, and old fashioned as I am, it is hard for me to accept the PH who turns out to be a woman. But then again she might be better then what I give her credit for. I hope she is strong enough to survive the "political" situation on this farm.

Who cares, we are here for eland antelope!

Our tracker is called Ambrosius, a long name for a short and skinny guy. He is also the driver of a brand new Toyota truck and shows us what the vehicle is able to do. Off and on we stop to take pictures of giraffes, zebras, gnus (wildebeest) and herds of springbuck. This farm is full of animals, and it does not take long for Ambrosius and Michael Fechter to spot a large herd of eland. If I would have to guess my number would have been higher then one hundred. Fechter points out some nice bulls, but with

100 animals you also have 200 eyes watching any approach. This is going to be a tough stalk.

James, Ambrosius and I have to stay back with the truck and a walky-talky to keep track of the herd's movement if possible, while Martin and Fechter disappear into the bush to start the stalk. The herd is more than one mile away, and we get ready for some serious waiting.

And waiting we are. About two hours later we spot Fechter and Martin for a brief moment. The herd is in motion and it seems to be hard for our hunters to get closer. Another hour before we hear a shot and another ten minutes before we hear Fechter on the walky-talky. He asks us about a big eland bull, but we are unable to see any wounded-looking animal and decide to meet at the point where Martin shot.

We do find a small blood trail and while Fechter and Martin try to outrun the eland herd with the truck and cut them off, Ambrosius, James and I work on tracking the bull down. Two different approaches hopefully deliver the outcome we all want.

And now we get an education in tracking one wounded eland bull within a herd of at least a hundred animals. Ambrosius is like a dog and never slows down. Ever so often he points to the ground to show us things that we do not see. This guy is strictly amazing to say the least.

James suffers under the heat and we have to slow down. We find hardly any blood and I wonder how an animal is able to digest a .470 N.E. slug and still follow the herd without falling behind. And that is when we hear another shot and another one. We hurry up and climb another hill. Another shot rings out while we are getting closer. We can see the Toyota truck but Martin and Fechter are gone. Another shot. The walky-talky comes to life and we hear the good news: "He [the eland] is down; we got him; he is down."

Moments later I see the first eland of my life from a close distance. What an animal that is that looks great and impressive even in death. An elegant monster with strong, spiraled stubby horns, a grayish coat and brown hair on the forehead — in my book this is the Goliath of the plains game.

Martin's pretty happy with his eland.

And there is my son with a big grin on his face that was not there two hours ago when I saw him being a little nervous. This was probably one of the most interesting stalks of his life, and he did all this just a few weeks after a major surgery. Once a Marine — always a Marine. I remember my older son Stephan going on an elk hunt in Wyoming with a cast on his leg. I guess my kids are no sissies!

It takes Martin, James and me a while to suck this all in and digest what we were allowed to experience: a good hunt with good company, a beautiful setting and most of all, a good outcome.

This eland antelope will be immortal from this day on, because a day like that will always be in our memory. A day like that makes you rich and sad at the same time, it makes you wonder if you will ever have a day like that again.

Eventually all the pictures are taken, we all had a shot of warm gin, the guns are empty and with a lot of muscle and a small winch we load the big antelope on the truck heading back to the Auas lodge, where a team of butchers seem to have been waiting for us. This is a lot of fresh meat that we are bringing in and nobody lets it go to waste.

We have another drink, some food, a good shower and an afternoon nap to get ready for a baboon hunt on the "monkey mountain."

Later Michael Fechter is driving us to a monster pile of rocks that might be sticking 600 feet out of the plains. I bet it would take you at least two hours to walk around it. This is the monkey mountain because the baboons like to come out of the plains in the evening and sleep at elevated places like that.

James takes position on the south side, Martin will cover the east slope and I walk up to the north side. I can see Martin; we wave at each other, get the guns loaded and wait. Wildebeest and a bunch of the dainty springbuck walk all the way up to me. Picture time, but not without the camera which I left in Fechter's car. Warthogs make their way through the tall grass, and a jackal is on the prowl.

No monkeys however.

The sun starts going down and I decide to leave my post and move over to Martin who starts waving at me. I stop in my tracks, put the binos up and see a bunch of baboons moving swiftly towards the southern hillside. A shot rings out and now all hell brakes loose. The baboons come our way. They are all over the mountain and do not really know what is going on. Martin operates the bolt of his 30/06 and fires. A baboon falls out of the cliffs. He shoots again and I do not even get my gun up. Obviously I am too slow for this game but I have only one shot and want to make it count. Martin should be out of ammo by now.

"You did not fire one shot Dad. What is wrong with you?" "I just did not get it together."

We climb down the hill and then I see him outlined against the evening sky: a big baboon sitting on top of the huge rock pile, watching us.

I open my gun and slide a 9.3 into the chamber. "Watch this, Martin." I take my time, push the double set trigger forward, adjust my sight picture one more time and slightly touch the trigger of my double. The 286 grain bullet slams into the baboon and knocks him off the cliff. I guess I can still do it.

It is getting too dark too quick, like always in Africa and so we empty the guns, forget about the baboons for now and make our way towards a set of headlights that approaches us. Katrin and Michael Fechter pick us up, James is a minute behind us and on the way back to the lodge our shots get longer and trickier.

We hit the bar at the Auas lodge, have good food, drink too much and talk too loud. We are happy and do not give a sh...

about the rest of the world. We had a great day — life is good for a change. And tomorrow we are going towards the Kalahari to a Farm called Nababis. If you are looking for a remote place, that is where we are going.

Michael Engster
Ponca City, OK

To be Continued...

Namibia 2006 —
Diary of a Hunting Trip, Part 2

I get up early and take a few pictures trying to capture the mood of an African sunrise. My next stop is the breakfast lounge where Michael Fechter and Martin are already waiting for me. Martin must be in a good mood and gets us laughing. Katrin who joined us too helps him while Jim Weber is sleeping in. We really get stuffed with all the good sausage, eggs, bacon, bread, coffee and fruit before we realize that we forgot one of the walky-talkies on the monkey mountain. Fechter starts up the truck and off we go. I know exactly where I left the damned thing.

Needless to say a big baboon is watching us when we get there, and needless to say we do not have a gun with us. Lucky baboon, I see you next time!

Back at the Auas lodge we get packed, load up our stuff and head south. Katnn is driving the "food" truck while we men drive the little Toyota 4x4 bus.

Stop at Rehoboth, the capital of the Baster homeland. The town is fairly clean, at least along the main road. We gas up and keep on trucking with Katrin leading. All the way through the Baster (bastard) homeland we see no game whatsoever. A few sheep, goats and cattle have replaced all native wildlife!! What a great conservation effort!

Our next stop is a settlement called Kalkrand, and what a place that is. The only persons working seem to be the guy at the little gas station and the barkeeper of the Kalahari Bar.

While Fechter and Katrin are getting gasoline, I take a peek into this bar and decide very fast to stay outside. This place is everything but inviting and the way the few guests look at me does not put me at ease. I back off.

We drive through the "village" and I am amazed how people can live on a dump site, and that is how the whole place looks like. Incredibly dirty, however all the people here seem to like it because nobody does anything but sit around small fires with a bunch of dogs, kids, goats and skinny horses running all over the place.

How they make a living remains an unanswered question. Fechter's explanations will not be repeated here.

The landscape changes, we are getting closer to the desert and the horizon is getting further away. Everything is green and not brown or red like expected. We want to see the desert and there is no desert. The desert was flooded four days earlier by a "once in a century" rain that washed out roads and destroyed some of the few bridges, and now we are standing here and wait for a bulldozer to push enough dirt back on the "road" to make it possible for us to cross the Fish River. It is hard for me to keep my cool watching the black guys work the heavy equipment. If you are in a hurry — do not go to Africa!

We keep on trucking along a dirt road that is as straight as it is endless. I am in the middle of an ocean of grass. Never before have I seen so much of nothing except in the Navy while being out on the Atlantic. I always loved the ocean, and I love this. All my life I was drawn to the outdoors and hated the contrived living of cities and the claustrophobic connivances of civilization that drive me to the vastness of places like this to fulfill some need of basic simplicity in myself. I had to steal these words, but they explain how I feel. And so I keep staring out of the window into a landscape I have only seen in my dreams.

Fechter slows down to make a left turn. A rusty sign says "Falkenhof which is the name of a more or less deserted farm that belongs to Fechter's brother. "Too remote to raise kids, and too dry to make a living. My brother is here only for a few weeks per year."

We cross a little stream, climb a hill and see another ocean of grass. "Three weeks ago this was all dry and red, not a leaf of grass on the ground. We did not have any rain for over a year, but now we are o.k."

We have to cross the same creek again, this time with some difficulty. The water is at least four feet deep. We learn that this river is called Packriemen Fluss, a name that goes back to 1904 when the German settlers started to make a new beginning in Africa just like other settlers did the same thing in the New World called America.

There is no road any more, just some narrow trail. After crossing the river for the third time some buildings show up on a grassy hill. "That is Nababis; that is the place". And then we drive through a gate into a big yard surrounded by some buildings and a lot of big cactus. This is the farm that Fechter's granduncle Gottreich Hubertus Mehnert, officer of the German Protection Troops, founded 1904, and that is the place where he died in 1967 at the age of 87 years. I will find more German history surrounding this place.

We are stiff climbing out of the car, some of Fechter's black people walk up to us and we are greeted in good old German. It always amazes me to hear completely "uneducated" people speak German, Afrikaans, English and their own native language on top of it.

Some fat, friendly woman shows us our rooms in the main building which is the oldest of them all. The rooms are small and sparsely furnished. A little closet, a chair and a bed, a door that does not close, a springbuck hide on the wall and a candle on the window sill, and that is it. I guess we do not need anything more.

It does not take long until we are asked to meet on the porch where the table is set and juicy eland steaks, salad and wine is waiting for us. It is nice to feel treated like a welcome guest in the middle of nowhere.

Katrin, the woman who never seems to get tired, suggests to go for a swim in the river and that is what we do. Swimming in the Kalahari Desert who is going to believe this one.

Well, it is a refreshing experience without crocodiles and snakes, and after sweating in the car for hours we let us soak in the "Packriemen Fluss".

Back at the farm we get ready for an afternoon hunt. Fechter's farm workers and their families are starving for red meat and they expect us to do our job" and deliver. Fechter wants to shoot some springbuck and so we pack only the little guns with the long reach. A.470 N.E. is the wrong medicine for long range shots on springbuck.

And so we leave the farm armed with a CZ bolt action rifle chambered for a.223 cartridge and a Sauer gun in 30/06. James however does not let go of his Ruger No.1 in.300 Win.mag.

There are springbuck everywhere but I can only guess they know what our intentions are and take off as soon as we get into a 300 yard range. Fechter, who seems to be able to see which one is young, old, male or female, drives like a maniac. It is a solid understatement to say that we get bounced around. This is a wild ride to say the least. Now he hits the brakes again seeing what I do not see. "Shoot the one to the left. Aim high, two inches over his shoulder." The springbuck is way out there hiding behind some sage colored brush. I fight the little gun that has a safety that works backwards, squeeze the trigger and nothing happens. You have to push the little lever back to get the gun into the ready mode. I have never seen this before, and needless to say the springbuck gets tired of posing and takes off. In the course of this pursuit that shakes our teeth loose, I miss the bugger three times listening to Michael Fechter's instructions about aiming high etc., before I turn my brain back on, remember something about ballistics and shoot the elusive springbuck straight through the right shoulder. The animal drops at the spot and I feel semi-redeemed.

There are springbuck everywhere...."

[and giraffe in the bush]

Fechter wants more meat, we load the antelope onto our truck and the race for meat continues. Deep inside I feel sorry when Jim misses with his first shot. We press on and Jim's second shot takes a good portion of the springbuck's neck off. These are all 250 to 300 yard shots. You have to get used to these distances and adjust.

Okay, we have another photo session with Jim's animal, we have another round of warm gin, and Martin overshoots another springbuck standing in a valley 280 yards from us.

Roaring laughter.

We decide to head back to Nababis. The Blue Hour is setting in and changes the colors around us like only Africa can do it. Warm, soothing, mysterious.

Our conversation dies down; we take pictures to capture the mood of the moment.

At Nababis the blacks are waiting for us and pull the two springbuck off the truck. Tonight the farm workers and their families are going to eat well and have a party. A while later we see the campfires glowing in the dark. Two big pots, one filled with meat, one filled with "I do not know what", are the center of attention.

Our meal consists of oryx sausage, lamb roast, fried potatoes, salad and wine. Candles and a campfire supply the light and let wild shadows dance in the big pepper trees above us while all kinds of birds, bugs, insects and other unknown critters create the background music.

Our conversation fits the night. Nobody spoils the moment discussing politics, religion, taxes, crime or global warming. We are here among friends and stretch the moment as long as we can. These are moments of inner happiness. We are blessed, and everybody seems to feel it.

One more glass of red wine.

3-8-2006

Fechter wakes us up while it is still dark. We brush our teeth by candle light and have a quick breakfast out on the porch where we meet Fechter's brother Horst who is quite different then Michael. He does not strike me as a goal getter, and his farm "Falkenhof" which we saw on our way in looked kind of run down.

After the second cup of coffee we push of into the bush. Some black wildebeest appear on a far off ridge, blue ones however we do not see. Jim Weber wants to go after his special friends, the baboons, and we drop him off. His plan is to stalk along the river going back towards the farm. We wish him luck; he might need it. The baboons are very smart and not easy to be approached. Sometimes I am tempted to think they know if you are carrying a gun or not.

Well, Jim Weber is in pursuit of his monkeys while we are still trying to spot some blue wildebeest. Fechter, who else, detects a sizable herd of black wildebeest with two blue ones in the middle. We are still far away, and I wonder how he can see these things. I guess he is good at what he is doing. I respect this guy and his calm and friendly way.

He stops the truck. 'Well Mike, are you up to some serious belly crawling?" Please note that this is not really a question but more like an order. "Hell yes, I was born ready. Bring it on buster." I am excited, and I am ready!

Martin stays with the truck, while the sage colored brush swallows us. It is hotter than hell; the shirt is soaked in no time and clings to my body. I see nothing but brush, rocks and thorns and try to keep up with Fechter who obviously knows which direction to go. We hit a small clearing, and looking around I get my bearings back. From now on we do the duck-walk and I feel like being in boot camp again. Fechter drops onto his knees. We can hear them before we see them. The wildebeest must have noticed something because they are all lined up looking in our direction. Then they start snorting and growling kind of like dogs. Just think about it: You are sitting in the middle of nothing else but thorns in the middle of nowhere and about 100 big black beasts are "growling" at you. Awesome, just awesome! My heart races, this is all a hunter can ask for, this is an adrenaline rush at its finest. This is the real thing! This is the poor man's buffalo we are after.

Two blue wildebeest slowly separate from the herd and move to our right. One of them is a very respectable old bull. We get into the super fast duck-walk, followed by the super fast regular walk, always trying to use the cover available to us. Sweat is running down my back, sweat is running into my eyes and makes them sting; my face is bathed in sweat, and sweaty hands hold the heavy rifle. My luck, this is by far the hottest day so far. The two bulls have stopped behind some heavy brush. They act nervous and might break into a run and be gone; however I do not have a clear shot. Fechter hands me his shooting stick. I am ready. Both bulls are looking at us. I have the crosshairs of my scope centered on the bull's chest and try to find a hole in the brush to shoot through. The wildebeest moves slightly and my cape gun kicks against my shoulder while the soft-pointed bullet finds its mark. This is an eighty yard shot, brush or no brush, and I do not miss at eighty yards.

The wildebeest jumps up high, turns around, walks three or four steps and goes down. Waidmannsheil. Trust me; I do not care how hot it is when Michael Fechter shakes my hand. I am a happy camper, 100 degrees Fahrenheit or not. "Good shooting, old man. Let's walk up to him and take a closer look."

And so I get to see the first blue wildebeest of my life up close. What an animal. I am standing in front of a magnificent bull and feel elated and sad at the same time. This bull is dead but will be alive in my memory as a rugged and majestic animal as long as I live.

I look around me and see miles and miles of grass and brush that looks as endless as the blue sky above us. I feel small, great, happy and blue; and I wonder how many more of these moments I am allowed to have before the journey is over.

Fechter seems to feel what is going on inside of me. "If you ever have to get away from whatever you want to get away from, you can stay on Nababis as long as you want, and I mean for free."

I shake his hand, mumble a thank you and walk away. My throat is tight.

In the meantime Martin has managed to get the truck through the brush and over the rocks and boulders. Fechter signals him towards us and like always, we have our photo session and a sip of warm gin.

Martin looks the wildebeest over to find my shot that left no exit wound. "Not too bad for an old man". Hell, I feel young right now and have been called an old man twice within ten minutes. Something is wrong here.

After a short discussion we decide that this animal is worth a shoulder mount. If you look at the photos, you will know why.

This is not a cape buffalo, but today that is what it is for me. The value of a trophy can not always be measured in inches or pounds.

The "old man" bags a wildebeest.

The spell this whole situation put on me slowly fades and reality sets in again. We have to get this animal out of the heat and so it gets loaded on to our trusted little truck. This happens to be another sauna session.

On the way back to the farm we try to locate James Weber. Doing so we see some spectacular country along the Packriemen River. I might have to think about Fechter's offer after all.

When we finally pick up a worn out baboon hunter we get to know that James saw a lot of these monkeys without ever getting a shot at one of them. He still had a great time and enjoyed himself greatly. He too shakes my hand on a great blue wildebeest while Fechter does his balls-to-the wall cross country 4-wheeling with the poor truck. And while the wildebeest definitely feels nothing any more, our teeth are getting loose from bouncing over rough terrain in breathtaking "Fechter speed".

Close to Nababis we pass the huts where the black farm workers live. They are all sitting around a fire, men, women, children and some scrawny looking dogs. To me it looks like they are having a good time, at least they laugh a lot and I envy them for the basic life they are living. Three of them jump on the fender of our truck and start butchering the wildebeest as soon as the vehicle comes to a stop at the farm. I have field dressed and butchered many game animals and watch these guys with professional interest. They are good and that is a fact. It does not take long and the wildebeest is just meat.

I go back to the old farmhouse to take a shower with semi-warm water. Afterwards I am sitting on the porch and enjoy this extremely remote and vast land where only a handful of people try to make a meager living.

From my elevated location above the Packriemen River I can see a sea of grass that stretches forever to meet a far away horizon. To my left are some reddish bluffs overlooking the brownish waters of the river and the only tall, deep green trees that grow along the banks. Patches of yellow flowers, purple and silver colored bushes as well as all shades of green and brown add to a painting that only nature is able to create. Further away, behind the river, the land rises slowly to a rolling prairie with dark thorn bushes growing in the ditches; while the rest is grass and more grass with white tips moving in the wind underneath a blue sky speckled with some white clouds drifting lazily in the breeze.

Looking down the hill I see the graveside of Hubertus Mehnert, which looks like a small chapel. I think I know why he never left this place for long.

And then there are the sounds of all the birds, the soft wind in the trees and the beating of your heart, and you feel intensively alive and very small and insignificant at the same time.

Slowly everybody comes to the porch, Katrin, Michael Fechter, James and Martin, and now we all listen to Fechter's monkey stories which are very interesting and sometimes strictly hilarious. I really like this guy, the way he handles himself and the way he treats his hunting guests. I like our conversations when nobody else is around and he allows a small look into his soul.

After a small snack prepared by Katrin and her black girls, we all try to take a nap which turns out to be more like another trip to the sauna.

Remember. No electricity — no air conditioning. I guess as of today I have a better understanding why the first settlers in my home state Oklahoma lived in dug-outs.

Lying on my little bed I feel the sweat pouring out of every single pore of my body. I am soaked to say the least and try not to think of the upcoming Oklahoma summer.

We climb back on our hunting vehicle at about 1600 hours (4 p.m.) and drive through a huge area covered with silver leaf brush. The big warthog that we spot a little late disappears before we can get a clear shot. Lucky Pumba!

Another river crossing, but this time the water looks deep and Fechter is nervous about getting stuck in the water. It would be a long walk home. "Hey Katnn, can you take your clothes off and walk through. I need to know how deep it is." Fechter must be joking.

"Sure thing Michael," and she strips down to her underwear and wades through the river while all the men either sit in the truck or in the back of it.

And so we follow Katrin to the other side where she greets us with her big smile. "That will cost you a drink or two tonight, gentlemen. I hope you did not take any pictures."

"We would never do a thing like this, plus we feel sorry that your cruel husband asked you to do a thing like that." Laughter.

Katrin climbs back on the truck and the search for another springbuck continues. Martin has switched guns. A Sauer&Sohn bolt action rifle in 30/06 replaced his .470 double which is definitely too much gun for a springbuck.

After a few wry long shots that only scare our prey, Martin stops listening to Fechter about holding high, puts the crosshairs of the scope in the middle of his target and we have a very dead springbuck. Waidmannsheil, we are done shooting on Nababis, load the little antelope up and drive back towards the farm. The evening colors are warm, and we have Fechter stop the truck various times to snap some pictures. Before we get close to home all the plains animals seemed to be lined up to say goodbye. We pass blessbucks, hartebeest, wildebeest, some kudus, warthogs as well as a bunch of ostriches while the baboons in the trees yell at us. What an evening.

Waidmannsheil, Martin!

The blacks are all outside sitting around their cooking fires, laughing and talking while the women stir whatever is in the pots, and the dogs are chasing the kids or the other way round. Two teenage boys get up as soon as they see us and jump on the truck. They want to butcher the springbuck—but more so they want whatever is inside like heart liver, lungs, kidneys and so forth. They eat it all.

And so we unload and let them get at it.

Soon afterwards we meet on the porch where one of the black women has a big fire going. Katnn and her girls prepare the food which is great like always. How they cook like that on an open fire amazes me.

Later on with candlelight and a dying fire setting the stage for stories and memories from the good old days I feel totally content. I do not miss the abundance of civilization we have to face every day and I do not miss all the entertainment we can have by just pushing a button not realizing that this kills our soul, dulls our brain and steals our imagination.

Here in the middle of nowhere I find peace.

After most of the wine is gone and only Martin and I are left on the porch we have a few father-and-son moments, priceless moments that allow us to let guards down and be who we really are.

Tomorrow we will be leaving this place and we might never see it again. Tomorrow we will drive back to the city with the crowded streets, the barbwire fences, the noise, the smell, the crime, the nice main road and the dirty, filthy slums. And by the way, there are no gleaming campfires in the city.

Tonight however the air is full of Africa, and we sit in the dark and talk.

Michael Engster
Ponca City, OK

To be Continued...

Namibia 2006 —
Diary of a Hunting Trip, Part 3

3-9-2006

We have breakfast on the porch while Fechter's farm workers are loading up the meat that needs to go to the slaughter house in Marienthal. We have a long ride ahead of us, and we have to make a few stops on the way back to Windhoek.

I feel sad to leave Nababis, but then again I always feel sad when I have to leave a remote place. And so we cross the Packriemen River two more times, dropping off some meat at the Falkenhof farm. Fechter's brother who owns this place is not like Michael. The place is definitely not inviting, and even the black guys are somewhat different.

We push on to Kalkrand to get gas and look at the Kalahari Bar one more time being surrounded by nothing else but filth.

I try to sleep on the way back to Rehoboth but I can not sleep in a car. And so I look out of the window to see the Baster Homeland where African animals have ceased to exist. Cattle, poachers, greed, stupidity and lack of any kind of game management have wiped this huge area clean of whatever Africa once had to offer. History repeats itself.

Fechter leaves the main road to drive through Rehoboth, the capital of the Baster land, but there is not much to see, however I have to admit that the place looks cleaner then I thought it would be.

Our next stop is the house of Fechter's parents that is hidden on a little hillside surrounded by cactus, huge flowery bushes and tall trees. We leave some more meat before we finally hit Windhoek.

Katrin who is leading the way drives up to a German restaurant called "Bierstuben", and that is where we have good German beer and a meal that is strictly outstanding. For a moment I feel like being back home in southern Germany. Needless to say — everybody speaks German, even the black waitresses. You figure.

The next stop is a taxidermy company called Nyatti Wildlife Art. I have seen many taxidermy shops in my days but this place is absolutely top notch. We drop some of our trophies off and look at the ones from last trip that are ready to be shipped to the States. The owner gives us a tour through his facility that employs at least 50 people and gives us a little story about his company. Interesting guy.

Now James Weber wants to see the Windhoek market and some of the sights, but he soon gets stuck with some naked girls from the Ovahimba tribe. He has to pay $5 US to have his picture taken before he is ready to browse the market where we all look for wood carvings. Fechter does the talking, knowing what the price structure has to be. We buy some nice stuff before we head towards the Protestant church and the statue of the German Horseman, a reminder of the few heroic soldiers of the Protection Troops of the early 1900.

Eventually we are done in Windhoek, which is really not such a bad city, and we drive towards Omunjereke.

The day is still young, and while Michael and Katrin stay on the farm to do some catching up with paperwork, telephone calls, etc.; James, Martin and Bernhard, the Herero foreman, go on a little baboon hunt.

I feel like being alone and make my way down to the river looking for frankolins and guinea fowl. My bird hunting trip however does not go as planned. The closer I get to the river, the higher the grass gets covering all the warthog holes. After falling into four of them my brain starts to work again. Here I am trying to break my legs, sweating and covered with spider webs. If there are any snakes I do not know, but in this tall grass I would not see them anyway. I can hardly see the warthogs running away from me, and I can definitely not get a shot at them. And so I leave the river bottom and make my way uphill.

I walk a lot this evening and being all by myself I feel that I own this part of Africa and all the animals within The vastness of the land makes you feel small, and at the same time it makes you feel like a king. Strange, is it not?

A lot of wildlife crosses my way and once I see a major warthog with long tusks sticking out of an ugly face. Luck is with the pig, I can not get out of the wind in time, and the fat Pumba disappears into the thorny brush while I start walking back to the farm.

The black clouds rolling in from north-west finally catch up with me, but I am still way too far from the ranch to even try to outrun the weather, and so I get a good African shower. When it rains — it pours and it does not stop. It also gets fairly cool, and back on the farm the Fechters decide to eat inside today.

Martin and James had as much luck hunting baboon as I had hunting birds and pigs. To compensate for that, we eat a lot and drink a lot this evening. We want to go to bed early, but jokes and hunting stories are exchanged, and all of a sudden it is late one more time. Good company does that to you.

3-10-2006

The birds wake me up again; I get out of the bed and step outside to see the sun coming up. I take a few pictures, unsuccessfully trying to capture the spell that this awakening day puts on me. A picture however is two dimensional. The third dimension, the noises and the smell of a new morning can not be captured by a digital camera, but only by your senses.

This is our last hunting day, and I do not want to be late for breakfast. I wake up Martin and James and walk over to the main house where Katrin and the black girls are busy preparing another gourmet meal.

We are not loosing any weight on this trip. No way, sir.

And while we are getting stuffed, the plan for the day is discussed. Fechter has to leave in the afternoon to pick up some Swedish hunters at the airport. In the morning Martin and James want to check for baboons, while I rather go on a little bird hunt. We all leave with our trusted 4x4 truck, and after a half-hour drive Michael Fechter drops me off on a small ridge. He shows me a windmill half way up on a far away hillside. "Can you see it? And when I nod he says: "It should take you about a good hour to get there. You find a tree stand and a waterhole. Good spot. We pick you up around noon. Good luck."

"Thanks, no sweat, I will be there."

And then I am alone. I get my gun ready and head for the windmill. I have more then four hours to get there. Piece of cake!

And so I watch the others disappear, put shells in my gun and start for the windmill. I am mesmerized by the landscape, the trees and flowers, the absolute abundance of birds and wildlife. The guinea fowl however are very shy today, and I can not get a shot. I can not get a shot at the warthog either, and still I feel great. I am all by myself again, and Africa belongs to me, the tall grass, the sandy creek beds, the wide valleys and the rocky ridges and the waterholes. The thing that does not belong to me is the windmill. The windmill disappeared on me and no matter how often or how long I glass the area, someone stole the damned windmill. If I put it in other words: I am lost.

And so I try to make my way back to where I came from which takes me about an hour and a half. Believe it or not, the windmill is back!

Now walking from ridge to ridge, from the big tree to the dead tree, from the red rock to the brush pile and so forth, I finally reach the windmill. I am as happy as I am tired and I look like a guy who took a shower with all his clothes on. And where is the compass when you need it?

Not even five minutes later I hear our truck. My buddies did not get a baboon, and it was easy for me to get here, and I have been waiting for them for over an hour.

Fechter looks at me and grins; I grin back. It was a good morning after all.

We slowly head back to Omunjereke. The baboons are still fooling us. Martin shoots twice with Fechter's Mauser 9,3x64 but unfortunately with little result. The same thing happens to me and my birds. There will be no guinea fowl soup after all.

Cheetah!! And three of them. "Someone shoot!" We know that Michael Fechter lost 8 calves the last month, and he lost them to these cats. He has a license from the game department and wants to see at least one of the cats dead. Well, Martin's gun is empty and Fechter has the spare shells in his pocket, my gun is also empty, and Jim Weber misses with his .300 Win.mag. The cats are gone. "Sh...!"

But what is this, one of the cats shows up again just to get killed by a well placed shot fired by our Yankee guest James Weber. We call it luck, he calls it shooting skills, but we are strictly joking. James is a good shot, and now he is also a lucky hunter. It does not happen too often to run into several cheetahs, miss and get a second chance. It does not even happen too often to just see these elusive cats. This is the real thing here; we are not in a park where animals pose for you.

The cheetah happens to be a young female which as of now is immortal due to the many pictures that we take.

The cat's hide however has to stay in Namibia due to the regulations that do not allow a hunter to bring such a trophy back to the U.S.A. Fechter finds his little whisky glasses and the gin bottle somewhere in the truck. A ceremonial drink is definitely on order, followed by a good glass of red wine back on the ranch.

And while we are sitting in the shade of the grass roof eating another one of Katrin's good dishes, we watch some warthogs fighting down at the bank of the river. It can hardly get any better.

Michael Fechter has to pick up new customers at the Windhoek airport and take them south to a Kalahari Desert hunt. It always hurts me to say goodbye to a friend, especially when you do not know when you will see him again. And so we make it short. "Take care, see you soon, keep your powder dry, do not let the bad guys get you, and so on." And then he is gone.

We have half a day of hunting left before our bags have to be packed. Thinking about the long flight back, the layovers, customs, security checks, waiting in line and eating sh...ty but expensive junk food at the airports makes my skin crawl.

One more time - if I could stay here, I think I would.

Bernhard picks us up at about 3.30 pm after we had a good cup of coffee. The farm feels empty without Fechter.

We are driving north, and I am the first one who is dropped off about 300 yards from a big tree stand. Martin and James stay on the truck. I watch them drive away until the African brush swallows them. My rifle is loaded when I slowly approach the tree stand. Seeing some movement out of the corner of my eye makes me stop. Too late, a big hog has spotted me sooner and is taking off double time. No chance for a shot.

Fechter told us to always check the tree stands for wasp nests and snakes. I can not detect either one and settle for some hours of waiting and glassing. It is like watching National Geographic on TV: springbuck, oryx, hartebeest, a sow with 5 piglets, a young jackal, some kudu cows and an assortment of birds keep me entertained; and when I finally spot a major warthog, adrenalin is released into my system.

The pig is about a mile away but makes good progress to come my way. I think about leaving my tree stand but abandon the idea. So far my sneaking up on pigs did not work — why should it work now. And so I watch this warthog for at least 20 minutes before I loose it in the tall grass. Obviously this is not my day, and the sow that brings her piglets right under my tree stand does nothing to improve this. I take some pictures before mamma pig takes her children back home. Nothing for the next hour. I would like to walk back to the ranch, but Bernhard wants to pick us all up and when you go hunting with other people one should stick to the plan.

Some of my springbuck friends that I have been watching ever since I got here start acting a little nervous. I reach for the binoculars and spot two warthogs about 50 yards out there, one of them sporting serious tusks. There is no time to waste. My cape gun comes up; I get the crosshairs centered and apply pressure to the front trigger, sending a 286 grain bullet on the way. The warthog dies in its tracks and my Africa hunt is over. This was a last-minute shot. The patience that was more or less forced on me paid of.

And so I get off the stand and walk over to the hog; I break a little branch and stick it in the warthog's mouth. This is an old German hunting tradition. The last bite. You have to respect the animals that you hunt. You can call it silly or laugh about this, but I will still do it.

(The final hour of our hunt; thank you Mr. warthog)

Death is not a dreadful thing in Africa not if you respect the animal you kill, not if you feed people or your memory.

Dragging the pig back to the trail turns out to be a job and a half. I guess it is a macho thing. I could have waited for Bernhard, however I have my own ideas about hunting. The more you work for a trophy, the more valuable it gets.

It is dark already when Bernhard comes back; we load up the pig, shake hands and go to pick up Martin and James.

On the way back to Omunjereke we swap stones. Martin shot a jackal with his .470 N.E. and we decide not to look at the pictures he took. James was baboon hunting and shot a fairly big one but could not find him in the dark. He was not really happy about this.

After a warm shower, supper with oryx filet, red cabbage, dumplings, salad, fruit and pudding accompanied by red wine from the Cape we have a few sundowners. The fire glows and our last evening slowly comes to an end.

3-11-2006

The last breakfast, good as always. I take the truck and drive back to my tree stand to pick up the binoculars that I forgot the night before.

Back on the farm we load up our gear, say goodbye and head for the airport.

"Goodbye to you Katrin and thanks for a good time. Hope to see you soon. Say hello to Michael!"

Needless to say, our flight to Johannesburg has been cancelled. People everywhere, all of them complaining, while the mess is getting bigger and bigger. Nobody knows what is going on. We feel sorry for the poor gate agent who is getting yelled at by almost everybody.

Whenever we stranded people get news through the loudspeaker, it turns out to be wrong. We watch some rich Texans bribing the gate agent with some good old American dollars. Shameful, but money talks.

A good hour later, after two planes could not start due to mechanical problems, things slowly get back to normal and we end up on the same flight the Texans paid money to get on.

I can not help smiling at them: "Nice to see you again, gents." They give me the dirty look in return.

The rest of our trip is boring and too long, like always. But finally we make it back to Ponca City. The next few days we have our photos developed and start talking about our next trip, much to the dismay of wife and mother.

But when you leave Africa, a part of you seems to stay there, and so you have to go back to reclaim it.

The times of Hemmingway's, Ruark's or even Capstick's safaris are over. Let us enjoy what is left as long as there is something left to enjoy!

Michael Engster
Ponca City, OK

Date: 2017
Location: Lephalale, RSA
Hunters: Martin, Amanda and Max Engster
            George Nix
            Sonja and Mike Engster
            Jean Lu Swart, PH

My wife is still sick but my new double rifle is regulated. How can you mention your wife and your rifle in one sentence ? Well, this is probably due to the fact that the weather is as bad as my mood. I tried to read Robert Ruark's book "Use enough Gun " but had to quit after a few pages and so I look at some pictures from our last vacation. Portugal was nice and interesting but this was not necessarily my type of vacation. I like to be with my old neighbors and friend from Germany, I like history and culture but I love places where nature has not been completely enslaved by man. May be that is why I live out in the Osage on Charlie Creek.

When I was a boy I was reading a lot of books about Africa and especially about safaris. Later when I joined the German Navy I got to see quite a few places but never Africa. Now I have about 16 safaris under my belt.

Unfortunately the "Safaris" of today differ from the safaris of the "good old days" when people have been out in the bush for months with little or no connection to the outside world. Todays safaris are more or less just hunting trips. You stay at a lodge, you go hunting for a few hours, you get pampered, full service, warm shower, may be a little campfire and a comfortable bed. The price tag for all this good stuff is directly tied to the star rated lodge and the African wildlife behind a game fence.

The old Africa is gone and it is gone forever !

A few things however are still left: Remote farms without game fences and without the luxury of fancy hunting lodges, places that have not yet been reached by total commerce. A few of them are still out there, hard to find but still there, and it is my quest to find them for the people I take on safari if you still want to use this word.

So where do we go next ? North eastern part of Namibia about 2 hrs east of the Grootfontein to a farm owned by Helmut and Margaret Friedrich. There we will be hunting with the bushmen for plains game.

And while I am looking forward to see these people again I look back to last summer when I had the adrenalin rush of a lifetime.

"Hey Mike, do you want to shoot a lion?" "My pocket book is too thin for that."

Jean Lu, our PH on this trip looks at me and replies: "I did not ask you if you can afford it, I asked you if you want to do it." I guess that caught my attention big time. And when you say — hell, yes — there is no going back, there is no changing your mind!

Jean Lu who got me into this told me we would have to wait a day or two for the local government officials to come up with the necessary paperwork to make it legal to take this unwanted lioness which was feeding on sheep and goats out of the cat population.

And so we waited hunting plains game in the meantime. My friend George who was talked into being my back up shooter for the lion hunt was exited while my wife Sonja was not so exited and I was getting a little nervous myself. We would not be sitting in a blind waiting for the bad cat to come to whatever bait — no, we would look for tracks with the help of some black guys and the walk the lion down until the moment of a final confrontation.

Well, and there will be no fence between us and a ticked of cat. I remember a hunting video with Mark Sullivan hunting lion with a young guy from RSA. As you might know his approach to hunting dangerous game is sometimes a little controversial because he is pushing the envelope. But the guy has guts.

And while we are waiting for the permit we continue hunting plains game as originally planned.

My grandson Max shoots his first Oryx while my son bags a very respectable waterbuck. Our good old friend George Nix, a 94 year old WW2 veteran who fought the Japanese on the Solomon Islands, shoots a big old warthog and an Impala ram while Sonja, Max and I try to get close to a Sable antelope to get a shot. After a while wife and grandson decide to stay back with the Toyota truck. Smart move.

I remember my shirt clinging to me, sweat running down my back into my pants, thorn bushes attacking me, and my rifle getting heavier by the minute. I quit quite a while ago to really notice my surroundings, I quit cursing the Impalas for giving our every location away. The only thing I see are the heels of the guy in front of me, and when he finally stops I kind of run into him.

"Sable", he whispers. "Over there." I wipe the sweat out of my eyes and see the black ghost sliding through the brush. My gun, a Heym bolt action rifle chambered in .375 H&H comes up and when the Sable steps out from behind its cover the crosshairs are lined up and I squeeze the Trigger. The bullet hits (you cannot really miss such a big target at about 90 yards), the bull makes three staggering steps and then it is game over.

Now I am not tired any more, I do not mind sweating any more, my legs do not hurt anymore and my gun feels lighter all of a sudden.. I am just a happy camper.

We shake hands, we admire the sable bull and give him the last bite (an old German hunting tradition), take pictures and have a schnaps and when the truck with my wife and my grandson Max shows up there is more shaking hands and taking pictures.

This was a hunting opportunity that I never expected and I notice that this is the first and last time I will ever be able to hunt a "Sable". My wallet is just not fat enough for a trophy animal like this.

But right now I cherish the moment and seeing that my wife Sonja and Max are happy for me makes my throat tight. On the way back to the Palala Lodge I relive this hunt over and over and in the evening the sable story is the topic of our campfire talk.

I am not heartbroken, I never planned shooting a lion in the first place. And to be honest — I am slightly nervous about this whole lion thing anyway.

We are sitting at the table having our last lunch and here comes Jean Lu. "Permit is here, we have to go right now !"

And so we grab our guns and climb onto the Toyota trucks while my wife asks me to be careful and we are on the road to the farm with the "bad" lioness that eats the wrong prey and scares the black population.

After about 45 minutes on bumpy roads that shake your teeth loose we reach a big iron gate where some people are already waiting for us. One of these guys is Hanno, the owner of this farm. I am 6feet and 3 inches tall and weigh 225 lbs but compared to Hanno I am a midget. This man, a gentle giant, is at least 7 feet tall and when we shake hands I have the feeling my fingers getting crushed.

Hanno gives us an idea about the situation with the lioness and the way we are going to approach the task on hand. We have 4 trucks with a tracker sitting on the hood or on the fender watching the sandy little roads for lion tracks. Contact between the cars is held via walky-talky, Whoever finds fresh pug marks has to report immediately and then the "game" will start..

And so we are slowly driving all over the place for about 1 hr. And there they are : Lion tracks ! Hanno shows up and lets us know that he was at this very spot about 10 minutes earlier without seeing any tracks at all — meaning our tracks are fresh.

"Come on boys, we are burning daylight." And so we follow the tracks. Jean Lu, my son and I are in front, two more guys are in the back while the government officials stay in the truck.

I am not nervous any more just totally focused. After just a few minutes the tracks curve to the right and then it happens. Africa means adventure, the chance to do things not possible any place else in the world, and here we are with a 'unfriendly" lioness less than 20 yards in front of us.

"Shoot"' whispers Jean Lu, but I do not need any coaching at this moment. It is strange how big a lion looks like when there are no steel bars between yourself and the cat.

My gun, a Heym .375 H&H comes up, the sights line up and pressure is applied to the trigger. The lioness jumps up, then goes down hard and for a mill second I feel like the great white hunter. I have no time to reload (my double rifle back home in Oklahoma would have been good at this moment) when the lion leaps into the thick bush to our right and George's gun goes off. I reload and then there is silence.

"Let's go and get the cat. I think your shot was good. What about your's, George?" "I was on it," George replies, and so we enter thicker brush with hearts pounding and guns ready.

What am I doing here? I am not a youngster any more. With 72 years under my belt you should be smart enough not to follow a wounded lion into the bush. You should be sitting on a campfire drinking a glass of wine telling big tales. But here I am doing something I only read about never thinking that I actually could be in the middle of it.

 Now everybody starts to talk, we shake a lot of hands and get ready for the "picture session" while the adrenalin level in my system slowly goes down to semi normal. Never in my life did I expect to go on a lion hunt. It just was financially out of my reach. I am happy to share such a rare moment with my son but as strange as it may seem — there is also some sadness in the mix.

The right front paw of the cat was obviously wounded by a snare. Poaching is rampant all over Africa.

May be this damaged front paw made the lion look for easier prey like goats and sheep. But goats and sheep are close to their owners and they could have been on the menu as well and so the lion had to go.

And one more time the animals lost being unable to fight the ever ongoing loss of their habitat.

Back at the lodge we tell everybody that we wounded the lion and have to go back out again the next morning to hopefully finish the job. The whole camp well knowing what that means drops into a somber mood. "Don't take it too hard Mike, things will work out tomorrow."

Finally someone spills the beans and the real lion story is getting told from different vantage points. It takes quite a while before the campfire dies down and — by the way—tomorrow we have to leave and go back home to Oklahoma. But one more time we take unforgettable memories with us, and these are the things that nobody can take away from you. These are the things that make you rich.

Feb. 22nd 2018

Here I am sitting in front of an open fire and watch the wild turkeys raiding my bird feeder in the yard.

I have all the paper work for 8 people as well as the gun permits from US customs in front of me. Tomorrow this "stuff" will be e-mailed to the police station at the Windhoek/Namibia airport. This is a new one for me but obviously it needs to be done. New regulations.

Like I might have mentioned before -Africa is like a cancer growth, it consumes you in a strange way. Today is my day to reflect. I look at old pictures and some Shutterfly books I made about previous hunts and feel the irresistible urge to go back to the black continent.

Right now I wonder what the 2018 safari to the northeastern part of Namibia will have in store for us.

My Guns

Tools of the Trade

Krieghoff Big Five double rifle
Cal.: .470 Nitro Express
Scope: Leopold 1.75–6 x 32

Krieghoff Drilling Trumpf
Cal.: 12 gage-12 gage—30106
Leopold Scope 2.5–8 x 36

Krieghoff Ultra
over + under rifle shotgun combination
Cal.: 9.3 x 74 R and 20 gage
Zeiss scope 3-9 x 40

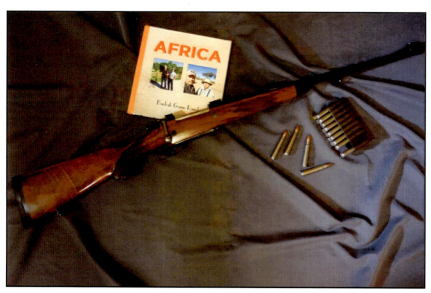

Mauser M98 Magnum
Cal.: .375 Holland and Holland Mag.

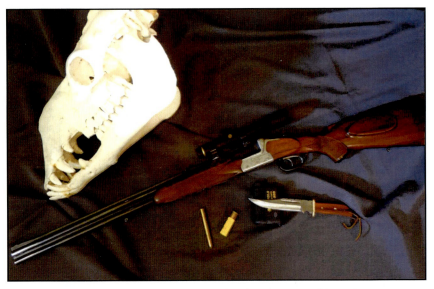

Heym over and under rifle-shotgun combination
Cal. 9.3 x 74R and 20 gage
Leopold scope 1.5-5 x 20

Merkel K3 single shot Stutzen
Cal. 30/06
Scope 3-10 x 42

Epilogue

I wrote this little book because I love hunting. I also love telling stories at a campfire, interact with people of different countries, different religions, different color, different education, different political views etc.

At a campfire we are all the same. The paint comes off and we are just people who escaped our all too political world for a brief moment. Campfire talk includes a little bit of bragging about our hunting experiences, trophies are getting bigger, shots get longer but other than that it is honest.

Hunting creates a bond between us, it creates understanding, tolerance and friendship.

In a time where a non functioning cell phone is a disaster, kids interact by texting only, games are played inside the houses and heroes are science fiction figures the contact to nature and the understanding of the outdoor world seems to fade away. In my mind this is a utterly sad as well as a dangerous development, and I hope that some of my stories might trigger a touch of interest in outdoor life.

Adventure is still out there but it is not found spending hours on the internet pushing buttons on a key board.

I also wrote this book for my children, grandkids and for all those who do not have the opportunity, the physical ability or just the drive to get out of the recliner and do what I did and still do. My hope is that they will get a inside look at a world that will eventually get smaller and smaller unless understanding of nature is rekindled.

And like I said before Adventure is still out there for those who dare!

Happy Trails
Mike Engster

Osage County
Oklahoma 2018

Epilogue

Summer 2018

I had to bring my wife Sonja to the airport in Oklahoma City. She wanted to see old friends back in Germany while I was about to take seven people to Northern Namibia for this year's safari.

On my way back to Ponca City, I started to feel bad and realized that my heart was out of rhythm one more time. They call it AFIB and it sucks. And so, I had a bad night but went to work the next morning after all. However, my heart said "NO" and so I pulled up in front of the ER at our local hospital at around 10.00 a.m.

They hooked me up to all kinds of good stuff, including an IV and tried to bring my heart rate down to normal, which seemed to be not quite that easy. Tough situations call for tough measures. They decided to stop my pump and start it again, and while I was talk to the doctor, they put me to sleep. Everything must have gone well, because I was sent home the same day just to be on a plane to Africa the morning after.

Still not feeling quite okay, I spent two day in a tent with "Nero" the dog of our African farmer Helmut Friedrich.

Namibia was beautiful like always, hunting was good but the political situation of the white farmers seemed to be deteriorating like always. The news out of the South African Union, the new land bill that can make whites homeless as we all the ever increasing number of murders (white farmers seem to be game) was especially disturbing.

I wonder where the black continent is going and I wonder what all the Chinese interests in Africa will create.

Back home things were not really good neither. My son, Martin, sent me a text asking me to call him as soon as I hit American soil. I was ready for bad news but not that; my cowboy friend, Sid Wilson, was shot to death with a .410 shotgun in the back at point blank range by his ex-wife, who committed suicide a few hours later. It is hard to imagine Sid not coming through our door any more, spurs jingling, having a cup of coffee and pancakes. It is hard not to hear him say—goodbye, madam—to my wife.

A tragic loss and what for?

But this was only the tip of the iceberg; August, a 20 year old girl who worked for my son had a car accident and died three months later after having been in a coma for quite a while. And then there was Jaden (21 year), who worked for us in the past, and she died just before she got married.

Sometimes I have a hard time to understand God's plans behind all this. But looking at the world around us, He just might be overworked and cannot see everything anymore.

And so, we continue living, trying to make the best of every day, dreaming of places where all things are good and in my case—planning another trip, looking for a bit of adventure as long as it is still out there and as long as I can physically do it because life Is not measured by the number of breaths you take but by the number of moments that take your breath away.

Happy Trails,
Mike Engster